ED YOUNG

THE REAL F WORD

FORGIVENESS
THE REAL F WORD

UNLEASHING THE POWER
OF FORGIVENESS

SMALL GROUP STUDIES

Published in Dallas, TX by Creality Publishing.

ISBN 10: 1-934146-01-3
ISBN 13: 978-1-934146-01-9

Cover Design and Layout: Jason Acker

CONTENTS

Small Groups are a vital part of how we do ministry at Fellowship Church, just as they are in many churches around the world. There are a number of different theories on how small groups should work and they are all great in different ways. The book you are holding is written with our model in mind. So take a minute to read the following explanation, then feel free to adapt as necessary.

Each of our small groups practices a three part agenda in every meeting. That agenda includes a social time, a discussion time, and a prayer time. Each of these elements share equal importance, but not necessarily equal time. To help you get the most out of this book we have included an explanation of each of the parts.

The first element of every small group meeting should be a time of socializing. This phase of the meeting should about 30% of your time together. Welcome everyone as they arrive at the host home, and make visitors feel welcome by introducing yourself and showing genuine interest in them. Enjoy some snacks, or if your group prefers, a meal together.

Then move on with second part of the meeting, the lesson. The lesson itself may take as much as 50% of your group's meeting time, but remember, it is not the most important element. You may want to start this phase of your meeting with a short "icebreaker" to get everyone talking. The questions in the "Start it Up" section of each chapter are what we refer to as "level the playing field" questions that everyone should be able to participate in, regardless of their level of spiritual maturity or Bible knowledge. As your group moves through the "Talk it Up" section in each chapter, remember that it is more important to finish on time than to finish each and every question. It is okay to skip some questions to be sure you allow enough time to take care of the third phase of the small group time: "Lift it Up."

The "Lift it Up" section is a vital part of every small group meeting and should be about 20% of the meeting. During this time you will be able to share with the group what God is doing in your life as well as asking the group to support you in specific prayers. To help focus this time, there are one or two questions at the end of each study that will prompt prayers based on the material you have just talked about. There is also a space for you to write down your prayer request(s) so you don't forget them and so you can communicate them clearly when it is your turn. Below that is a place to write down the prayer requests of the people in your group so you can remember and pray for each request throughout the week.

As an additional tool to assist you in your journey of spiritual development there is a "Step it Up" section at the end of each session. This section consists of five devotional thoughts that reinforce the lesson you've just completed and are designed to help you develop a regular quiet time with God. To get the absolute most from this study I challenge you to take five or ten minutes a day to read and apply these devotionals to your life. If your group meets twice a month or bi-weekly, choose five of the intervening days to incorporate these thoughts into your devotional life.

In select studies, we have incorporated special notes for youth groups using this material. You will notice a special icon Ⓨ used several times in each session. This indicates that there is a comment or question especially for youth included in the leader's guide for that part of the study. When you see that icon, simply turn to the leader's guide for that session in the back of the book and find the corresponding Ⓨ and letter (for instance, Ⓨ-a). These notes are designed to help each discussion time speak to the unique needs and issues of youth.

FORGIVENESS

Not too long ago, I was having a discussion with a friend and things got a little heated. There were some things, some hard things, I needed to say to this person, but I didn't say them in the best way possible. I don't regret what I said—everything I said was appropriate and needed to be addressed. But I do regret how I said it. When God started pointing out the error of my ways, I was reluctant to address it. But he convicted me and prompted me to go back to this friend and ask for forgiveness. I didn't want to do it. It was uncomfortable and awkward, but seeking forgiveness from this person was a necessary step to restore our friendship and to restore my relationship with Christ.

Forgiveness is the cornerstone of the Christian life. Because of the death, burial and resurrection of Jesus Christ, Christ-followers are completely and eternally forgiven from their sins. Christians celebrate the fact that a holy and righteous God died in our place, wiping the slate clean in our lives. We gravitate towards the biblical stories like the prodigal son who was completely exonerated from his selfish and stubborn rebellion. And we count on the fact that we can offer up a microwave prayer at anytime, anyplace to access God's gift of forgiveness.

Forgiveness feels great—as long as we are the beneficiaries. But like almost everything in life, there are two sides to the coin when it comes to forgiveness. We like being forgiven, but it's not very fun when you have to ask for forgiveness.

Or what about when we, as the offended, are asked to forgive someone else? We rush to be forgiven of our offenses, but we balk when it's time to forgive someone who has offended us. When someone has hurt us, we don't want any part of the forgiveness equation. We'd rather retaliate than release the offender.

Through this study, we will discover God's powerful truths about this highly-charged subject of forgiveness. We will discover the amazing benefits that come with forgiveness—both for the forgiven and the forgiver. And we will see how God can use "The Real F Word" to radically transform our lives!

FORGIVENESS

COLLATERAL DAMAGE

START IT UP

A couple of weeks ago I was at a gas station. While I was filling my car, I saw this guy jogging with a monstrous Doberman Pinscher on a leash. I love dogs, so I was checking this scene out pretty intently.

The guy ran past me with the dog and stopped and began to tie the dog's leash to a bench just outside the front door—one that was anchored in concrete. After he tied the Doberman to the bench, he went inside to get something to drink.

All of a sudden, something spooked this dog. You could see the whites of his eyes as he made a mad dash toward the busy freeway. He took off with such force, with such torque, that he ripped the bench out of its cement supports! And as the Doberman took off dragging this bench behind him, sparks were flying everywhere. I remember thinking, "This dog is going to get smashed! He's going to get hit!"

Cars all over the road screeched to a stop. And as the dog ran towards a SUV that was turning left, the bench was barreling down. The dog stopped; the bench didn't. Instead, it kept going and slammed right into the side of the SUV. BAM! Parts went flying. Then the dog turned and ran towards a Volkswagen® behind the busted SUV. Once again, the dog stopped short, but the bench did not. SLAM...right into the Volkswagen! The owner of the gas station came running out of the store, chasing the dog while the dog's master came out spilling Gatorade® everywhere trying to catch them both. I couldn't believe it!

1. What is the most outrageous event you have witnessed?

_____

_____

_____

_____

TALK IT UP

When it comes to today's subject matter, The Real F-Word, a lot of us are like that Doberman. We are leashed up to anger, resentment, and unforgiveness. We don't realize it, but we are dragging it all through life and it's causing some serious collateral damage in our relationships. It's damaging the potential God has for us and it's smashing up innocent bystanders who happen to get caught in our wake.

UNLEASHING UNFORGIVENESS IS UNNATURAL Ⓨ-a

I've discovered something about the real F-word. Forgiving someone, or you could say unleashing unforgiveness, is unnatural. The bottom line is I don't like to do it, and you don't either. When someone hurts me, when someone damages me, when someone says something against me; I like to hold a grudge. I want to get back at them. When someone tells me I should forgive them, I don't like it because it flies in the face of every natural instinct I have.

2. Why do you think it is so unnatural to forgive someone who has hurt you?

_____

_____

_____

_____

I want you to think about something over the next several moments. Who is sitting on your bench? Could it be an ex-spouse, a parent, a coach, or someone who did something to you that no one really knows about except that person, yourself and God? Maybe someone messed you around in the business world or has said some hurtful things to you at school. Who is sitting on your bench?

3. Without being specific, why are these people on your bench?

_____

_____

_____

_____

Do you realize when we harbor unforgiveness we're saying, "Okay, you control my life. I'm the puppet. You've got the strings. You hurt me. You ruined my life. You keep me from all this potential." That's what we're saying when we remained leashed up to unforgiveness. Ⓨ-**b**

I've lived that way before, and it's no way to live. Years ago a man hurt me and my parents deeply. For two years I remained leashed up to unforgiveness. I kept telling myself, "I'm going to make this guy pay. I'll get him back. I'll show him!"

I was leashed up to unforgiveness until something supernatural happened. God gave me the strength to get over it. And he can do the same for you too. Jesus talked about getting unleashed in Matthew 18.

Jesus had been talking about the real F-word. Simon Peter was listening and must have been dealing with unforgiveness in his life. He made some serious assumptions about forgiveness—assumptions that were wrong, but assumptions that we have all made.

> _Then Peter came to Jesus and asked, "Lord, how many times shall I forgive my brother when he sins against me? Up to seven times?" Matthew 18:21_

Check out the tenor of that question. Simon Peter is trying to show off because during that day, rabbis (Jewish teachers) taught that if you forgave someone three times, that was monster forgiveness. Here's Simon Peter saying, "Hey Jesus, I am a disciple. I'm a spiritual stud. How about I prove my maturity by forgiving somebody who hurts me seven times? That's pretty amazing, isn't it Jesus? I mean, isn't that phenomenal?"

4. Imagine you found out someone in your life had spread some nasty lies about you. If that person came to you and asked for forgiveness, what would you do?

_____

_____

_____

_____

5. What if that same person kept spreading lies about you? How many times do you think you could offer that person forgiveness?

_____

_____

_____

_____

Simon Peter made the wrong assumption. He thought forgiveness was strictly for the person who did the crime, the person who was the offending party. **But forgiveness is more for the one who has been offended than the one who has carried out the offense.**

A lot of us think forgiveness is more for the person that hurt us, but that is not true. Forgiveness is more for us. Simon Peter didn't get it so Jesus launched into one of his classic stories.

> _Therefore, the kingdom of heaven is like a king who wanted to settle accounts with his servants. As he began the settlement, a man who owed him ten thousand talents was brought to him. Since he was not able to pay, the master ordered that he and his wife and his children and all that he had be sold to repay the debt. Matthew 18:23-25_

If you take the amount of money this servant owed this king and put it into today's money, this servant owed $10 million. That's a lot of money. So when the king called this guy into his palatial office and said, "It's payday," you know the borrower was in serious trouble.

Back then you couldn't file Chapter 11 or Chapter 13 bankruptcy. People that couldn't pay up could be sold into slavery to repay the debt. Read on to find out what happens to the servant.

> *The servant fell on his knees before him. "Be patient with me,"*
> *he begged, "and I will pay back everything." The servant's master*
> *took pity on him, canceled the debt and let him go.*
> *Matthew 18:26-27*

Now this king could have put the servant and his entire family on the auction block. But he didn't. Instead, this wealthy guy did something that was completely unexpected. He canceled the debt. Can you imagine owing $10 million and then having your debt forgiven on the spot? That would be a serious party!

6. How do you think you would feel if you were late on a few mortgage payments and your mortgage company called you up to say, "Don't worry about it. We'll take care of the rest you owe"? (Y)-c

_____

_____

_____

_____

You would think this forgiven servant would be in the forgiving spirit after his massive debt was forgiven. You would think the servant would be in such a great mood over what was done for him that nothing could bring him down. You would think that...

> *But when that servant went out, he found one of his fellow servants*
> *who owed him a hundred denarii. He grabbed him and began to*
> *choke him. "Pay back what you owe me!" he demanded.*

COLLATERAL DAMAGE FORGIVENESS

His fellow servant fell to his knees and begged him, "Be patient with me, and I will pay you back."

But he refused. Instead, he went off and had the man thrown into prison until he could pay the debt. When the other servants saw what had happened, they were greatly distressed and went and told their master everything that had happened.

Then the master called the servant in. "You wicked servant," he said, "I canceled all that debt of yours because you begged me to. Shouldn't you have had mercy on your fellow servant just as I had on you?" In anger his master turned him over to the jailers to be tortured, until he should pay back all he owed.
Matthew 18:28-34

The amount the forgiven servant was trying to collect was around $11. Just think about that. He was just forgiven a debt of $10 million and he was ready to fight over $11. The king delivered this greedy servant from prison, and now, because of $11, he put himself back in prison.

The same is true in your life and mine. We've been completely delivered as Christ followers. We've been set free. We've been forgiven. The debt's been taken care of. But when we harbor unforgiveness, we're putting ourselves back in prison. We're leashing ourselves back to the condition we had before we understood and appropriated the forgiveness of Jesus Christ.

When someone has hurt us, when someone has trashed us, when someone has taken advantage of us, we feel like there is a debt that has been created. We think, "They owe me. They need to pay." And too often, we act like the first servant and try to make those who have offended us pay. We forget how much we have been forgiven and we hold on to the little debt.

7. Why do you think we so easily ignore how much we have been forgiven when it is our turn to offer forgiveness?

_____

_____

_____

Jesus finishes his story with a scary warning. I wish this verse was not in the Bible. I wish I could take some white out, and erase it. It's so convicting and it messes me up. Here's how Jesus summarized this story:

> *This is how my heavenly Father will treat each of you unless you forgive your brother from your heart. Matthew 18:35*

This guy had received forgiveness, but he hadn't really experienced forgiveness in the depth of his being. Because he hadn't really experienced it, he couldn't share it with others. I think we've all been in the same boat. We've received forgiveness from Jesus, but we've not really embraced it in the depth of our being. And because of this, we can't share it with others.

Here's what the Bible is saying. If we harbor unforgiveness toward others, if we are leashed up to the resentment and the animosity and the pain, God will hold us accountable. I wish it was not in there, but that's what the Bible says. If we refuse to forgive, we will live on a treadmill of torture. Can you imagine trying to run on a treadmill while you are leashed up to a bench with four, five, six or seven people on it? That's the picture that Jesus was trying to paint for us.

8. When you think about how God has forgiven you, how does it make you feel about the unforgiveness you are leashed to?

_____

_____

_____

_____

Let's go back to Simon Peter's question that sparked this entire story. Simon wanted to know if forgiving someone seven times was enough. Read Jesus' response.

> *Jesus answered, "I tell you, not seven times, but seventy-seven times." Matthew 18:22*

The number seventy-seven is intended to be an illustration of forgiveness over and over again. Jesus told him that he was to offer forgiveness beyond what he could count. Jesus was teaching that forgiveness should be a habit, part of our lifestyle.

Some of you are thinking, "Well, you don't realize what's happened to me. You don't realize what my father did. You don't realize what my mother did. You don't realize what my uncle did or my friend or whoever. You don't realize what that coach said to me. For me to forgive them would be to minimize what they did to me. I'm not going to let them off that easy. I'm going to make them pay. I'm going to make them suffer."

You're right; I don't know what you've gone through. But, forgiving someone doesn't mean you are minimizing their behavior. I don't know what they did to you. And you don't know what people did to me. Only God knows, and he tells us to cancel the debt, to forgive them. We're not minimizing what they did. We're freeing ourselves up. We're giving ourselves a gift that money can't buy.

Think about the word "forgiveness." It has the word "give" in it. When we forgive, we give ourselves the ultimate gift. Also, we're giving the other person who messed us around a gift. We're *giving* them room to change. So don't play the "I'm-going-to-get-you-back" game. Cancel the debt as Jesus did for you. Say, "You're forgiven."

Unforgiveness is really hard because we like to hold onto it for some reason. It can be fun. It can give us a rush. But God says, "By my power and my grace, I want you to do something that swims against the current of your instincts, something that flies in the face of everything you want to do naturally."

That's why unleashing unforgiveness is unnatural. And to go a little bit deeper, the reason we have a tough time with it is because we're selfish human beings. We think life is all about us. And this attitude plays a huge part in putting up barriers that keep us leashed to the bench of unforgiveness.

THE SELF-DECEPTION BARRIER

Pride is one thing, but we also rationalize our way out many times. In other words, we tell ourselves lies. We say, "What I did to that person is no big deal. They totally overreacted. They're an emotional basket case, anyway. It wasn't that big of a deal. It was a long time ago." Or we say, "What my mother did to me.... Yes, she was an alcoholic, but it didn't really affect me. I've swept it under the rug. It doesn't affect me. What that coach, what that teacher said to me during my childhood.... The stuff that happened doesn't really affect me today. Everything's fine in my life. I'm fine." Be very careful. That's a barrier that will come back to hurt you.

9. How have you seen someone stay leashed to unforgiveness because of a self-deception barrier? Ⓨ-d

_____

_____

_____

_____

THE SELF-DEFENSE BARRIER

Another barrier is the self-defense barrier. That's the one that we love. We say, "I'm going to get you back. You messed me around. You hurt me, so I'm going to get you back."

For twenty-four months, I harbored the same kind of thinking with that guy that hurt me and my parents. "I'm going to get this guy back. I'm going to make him pay. I'm going to show him. Revenge! I'm going to take care of it." Ⓨ-e

Have you ever stopped to realize this: Forgiveness is a great act of faith? It's When we say, "Debt canceled. I forgive you. I release you," we're really saying, "God, you are the ultimate judge. God, I give the situation to you. You are going to take care of this person better than I can. God, I trust you."

Do not take revenge, my friends, but leave room for God's wrath, for it is written: "It is mine to avenge; I will repay," says the Lord. Romans 12:19

10. What could you do to help you trust God and give him control of the person who wronged you?

_____

_____

_____

_____

THE SELF-IMAGE BARRIER

There's another barrier—the self-image barrier. We say, "Hey, if you think I'm going to admit that I was wrong or I'm going to admit that they messed me around, you are wrong. I'm up here and I'd have to lower myself to do that."

Actually, we are at our strongest when we admit the obvious to God and to others. We are in a great position of strength and influence when we say, "Debt canceled. I forgive." Don't let the self-image barrier keep you from unleashing your unforgiveness. This barrier is really all about your pride. It is a desire to make yourself look stronger and better than others. When those feelings creep in, take them to God. Define your self-image on God's terms and you won't have to fight for it on your own. Ⓨ-f

THE SELF-PROTECTION BARRIER

Here is our final barrier—the self-protection barrier. A lot of you are breaking out into a cold sweat just thinking about having to do the work of forgiveness that needs to be done. You get nervous thinking about sitting across the table from someone that you are in conflict with. It makes you sick to think about sitting in someone's family room and saying, "I was wrong. Will you forgive me?" Don't let it keep you from being unleashed. Ⓨ-g

Unleashing unforgiveness is unnatural. I know that as well as anyone. But God wants to do this amazing work in your life. God wants to release all of us so we can discover the freedom, the joy and the amazing love that he has for us.

You might still be wondering what happened to the Doberman. The owner of the gas station ran out into the street. The dog owner ran out, spilling Gatorade®

everywhere. And when the Doberman saw his master, he completely relaxed. The master grabbed the leash, untied it from the tattered bench and led the Doberman to safety.

The picture of the Doberman and his master is what God wants to do in your life throughout this study. He wants to bring to your mind those names, those faces, those scenarios and situations you're holding on to. If you'll stop long enough to look to him, your Master will untie you and lead you to safety.

If we could see the amazing place where God wants to lead us, we wouldn't believe it. I'm talking about physically, spiritually, emotionally and relationally. That is the power of the Real F-Word—forgiveness.

WRAP IT UP

Take your hands and make a fist as you bow your heads for a moment. So often in my own prayer life, I've found it vital to do something physical as a reminder to me and God that I'm serious about doing what I'm praying. I want your clenched fist to represent something you're holding on to. What kind of unforgiveness are you holding on to? What kind of resentment, what kind of anger are you dealing with? Do you know what the word forgive means in the Bible? It means to release. Do you know what the word resentment means? It means to feel again. So many of us are feeling again, and again, and again the pain and hurt from what that person has done to us. We're playing our own movie clips of the hurts we're holding on to. It could be that person seated next to you. It could be someone you'll see tomorrow morning at work. It could be a family member. It may even be someone who passed away a long time ago.

Right now, as a physical sign to ourselves and to God, release your fists and say, "God, I forgive them. I release them. Debt canceled." Quietly tell God, "I'm not minimizing what's happened. I'm just doing what you want me to do so I can discover the best you have for me. God, you have an awesome agenda that you want to lead me through and I know the only way to do it is by living a life of forgiveness. God, unleashing unforgiveness is unnatural. But because of your power, I open up my hands to you."

Right now God is doing some wonderful things in all of our lives. Thank him for all those things that come to mind. And over the next several weeks we're going to talk about forgiveness in an even more profound and deeper manner as we discover the benefits, the beauty and the richness of this whole concept of forgiveness that comes from God.

Prayer Requests:

_____

_____

_____

_____

_____

_____

_____

_____

_____

_____

_____

_____

_____

_____

_____

_____

_____

_____

Notes:

_____

_____

_____

_____

_____

_____

_____

_____

_____

_____

_____

_____

_____

_____

_____

_____

_____

_____

_____

_____

_____

_____

_____

_____

STEP IT UP

Take a step further over the next few days and spend some time reflecting on the following devotional thoughts that reinforce the previous session. Use these as reminders to take what you've learned and apply it to your everyday life.

DAY 1

Matthew 18:21-22

Do you know anybody who always takes it a step further than you were willing to go? When you play a simple prank by taking their stapler, this person retaliates by hiding everything in your office. You want to do something nice for your friend so you stop by the grocery store and pick up cookies; the other person shows up with an exotic, homemade dessert. You buy two boxes of Girl Scout® cookies to be nice, they buy twenty. Some people are just like that.

Jesus had a habit of taking things to the next level. One of the most prominent examples of Jesus taking it to the next level is in Matthew 5. Jesus went from topic to topic covered in the Old Testament, and then set the bar even higher. Laws of the Old Testament were expanded and upgraded in his teachings. The result was a way of life proclaiming love instead of just laws.

Today you read another example of Jesus taking it to the next level. Peter thought he was raising the bar by offering forgiveness 7 times instead of the required 3 times. Peter was offering much more forgiveness compared to what the religious leaders of the day prescribed. Then Jesus stepped it up even further. Depending on which translation of the Bible you read, Jesus said forgive "seventy-seven times" or "seventy times seven." The exact number was not the point Jesus was trying to make. The point was that forgiveness should be an abundant act that should not be measured.

When Jesus stepped up the expectations, it usually flew in the face of his culture. Jesus had a way of asking more than what society expected. Society expected you to forgive several times. Jesus asked you to forgive without limits. That might seem like a lot to ask, but don't forget the sacrifice that Jesus made for all of us. Society wanted a savior that wore a crown. Jesus brought salvation by hanging on a cross. He went much further than people expected to prove his love for mankind.

Are there any situations in your life that need the work of forgiveness that society would ignore? In other words, are there any relationships in your life needing forgiveness that Jesus expects you to handle differently than what society tells you?

Notes:

_____

_____

_____

_____

_____

_____

_____

_____

Prayer Requests:

_____

_____

_____

_____

_____

_____

_____

DAY 2

Matthew 18:23-33

A noble cause can become an excuse for doing something that is illegal or socially taboo. A driver who is speeding and weaving in an out of traffic is normally pulled over, but if this behavior is due to a pregnant passenger on the way to the hospital, the perception changes. Punching someone can lead to assault charges, but punching someone in defense of a loved one is somehow considered noble.

As Christians, we are asked to defy societal expectations in the name of forgiveness. When we forgive others, we are forgoing what others expect from us. Our friends and coworkers expect us to exact revenge. They expect us to get even. In a world where forgiveness is socially taboo, Jesus asks you to cross that line for a noble cause.

But Jesus is not asking you to do anything he has not done. Jesus deserved apologies from the many who wronged him. He deserved those who wronged him to take the first step. Jesus would have been within the socially acceptable bounds if he had waited for those who wronged him to take the initiative. He could even be excused if he traded insults with the religious leaders of his day. However, Jesus crossed the line. His bold behavior made forgiveness available to us.

Forgiving someone or going to a person and asking for forgiveness will be socially taboo. You will have to cross social lines to accomplish your mission. Let me challenge you to cross those lines boldly as Christ did. Cross them knowing you are acting on the words of Christ. You have a noble cause. You are forgiving because you have been forgiven.

Imagine someone does not understand why you are forgiving the person who wronged you. Explain why you offered forgiveness even when it is not the social norm.

Notes:

_____

_____

_____

_____

_____

_____

_____

_____

Prayer Requests:

_____

_____

_____

_____

_____

_____

_____

_____

_____

_____

_____

DAY 3

Matthew 18:34-35

It would be nice if we did everything out of the right motivation, but we don't. Most people don't pay their taxes because they want to finance the goals of the current President. They pay their taxes because they don't want special attention from the IRS. Most people don't drive the speed limit because they believe it is better for the environment and safer for others. They drive that speed because there could be highway patrol around the corner. Doing everything out of the right motivation would be nice, but it doesn't always happen.

Yesterday we discussed the noble reason for forgiving others. Jesus forgave us so we should forgive others. That is the type of reasoning that gives you a warm, fuzzy feeling knowing that you did the right thing. Today is about the not-so-noble reason. If we don't forgive others, God is coming for us. Today's reasoning has more of an IRS or highway patrol effect.

Forgiving others because God will discipline you if you don't will not give you warm and fuzzy feelings. You won't even get the same rewards for doing the right thing when you do it out of compulsion. Acting out of fear may not earn you the most treasures in heaven, but it will help you escape consequences in the present.

God is serious about forgiveness. He wants us to fully comply. He compels us to forgive out of the beautiful sacrifice Jesus made for us. But if that does not work, he will prod us towards forgiveness with the threat of his wrath. In both cases, he asks us to forgive because it is best for us. In the end, it may not be noble to forgive just because you are afraid of God, but God can use your obedience to change your motivation.

If you are struggling with obeying from the right motives, ask God to help you embrace the love he has for you so you can use it as a motivation for your obedience.

FORGIVENESS

Notes:

_____

_____

_____

_____

_____

_____

_____

_____

Prayer Requests:

_____

_____

_____

_____

_____

_____

_____

_____

_____

_____

_____

DAY 4

Romans 12:19

At some point in your life (and it might be right now) there has been someone you struggled to forgive. Why? There are the obvious, surface level answers to the question, but dig deeper. What is the true source of your inability to forgive? One answer might surprise you.

Unforgiveness can be a symptom of not trusting God. The reason you cannot release someone who hurt you is because you do not trust God. If you forgive that person for messing you around, who will punish them? If you forgive that person when they embarrassed you, who will restore your dignity? If you forgive the person who took advantage of your trust, who will protect you the next time? The answer is God. God is the righteous judge that can be trusted. But we must apply that trust to motivate us towards forgiveness.

Forgiving others is about more than just letting go of that person's offense. Asking for forgiveness puts you in a vulnerable position. When you open up, who will protect you? The answer is God. If you trust him and act obediently, you can be sure that he will be there for you. This does not mean every forgiveness situation will work out just as you wanted, but it does mean God will be there for you through it all.

Asking for forgiveness and offering forgiveness are both related to trusting in God. Show that you trust God by offering the forgiveness or asking for forgiveness as he desires.

Think of the forgiveness issue you struggle with the most. Is your obstacle in any way related to your trust in God?

If your obstacle is trust related, ask God to help you remember how trusting him in the past has benefited you.

Notes:

_____

_____

_____

_____

_____

_____

_____

_____

Prayer Requests:

_____

_____

_____

_____

_____

_____

_____

_____

_____

_____

_____

DAY 5

1 Corinthians 2:4-5

If you were going to make a life-changing presentation, what would you do? Would you employ the latest and greatest technology to create moments of amazement? Would you gather great artists together to dream unique ideas of creativity? Would you have the best speech writers in the world carefully craft every word until you were convinced you had the persuasiveness to change the minds of your listeners? There are many options, but the Apostle Paul chose none of these.

Paul went to the Corinthians to tell them about Jesus, but he did not employ the latest and greatest tricks of his day. He worked hard and presented the message with diligence, but he relied on the power of God to change minds, and ultimately, change hearts. Paul knew that fancy techniques without the power of God would only disappoint the Corinthians. The only proven strategy was to give them the truth about God.

We could learn a lot from Paul's ministry. Any discipline or fortitude we possess will never match the power of God. When it comes to unleashing unforgiveness, it is unnatural. On our own power, we will fail time and time again. That is why we must rely on the supernatural power that is from God. Only by God's strength will we be able to accomplish what comes so unnatural to us.

Identify an area of unforgiveness you are dealing with, and ask for God's supernatural power in that area of your life.

Notes:

_____

_____

_____

_____

_____

_____

_____

_____

Prayer Requests:

_____

_____

_____

_____

_____

_____

_____

_____

_____

_____

FORGIVENESS

FORGIVE FOR GOOD

START IT UP

Forgiveness can lead to freedom.

A woman in her mid-50's walked up to me a couple days after I taught on forgiveness with tears streaming down her face. She said, "Ed, I want you to know something. I've been praying that God would teach me about forgiveness." She said, "My husband has left me and moved in with another woman. Because of Scripture and specifically because of your talk from Matthew 18, I'm finally free for the first time in ten months!" **(Y)-a**

1. How have you experienced freedom from unleashing your unforgiveness?

_____

_____

_____

_____

TALK IT UP

Last time we learned that unleashing unforgiveness is unnatural. I don't like to do it, and you don't either. Releasing someone, forgiving someone and canceling the debt flies in the face of every instinct we have. When someone's hurt me, when someone's messed me around, I want to get them back. "I'll make them pay," I say. "I'm going to do something to get them."

UNLEASHING UNFORGIVENESS IS UNBELIEVABLE

Today, as we go deeper into this whole forgiveness concept, God is going to show us that unleashing unforgiveness is truly unbelievable. Being leashed to unforgiveness can mess up not only present day situations and circumstances, but also those in the future. The moment you harbor a hurt, resentment or unforgiveness, you're saying to that person, "You control my life. I don't want to control my own life. I don't even want God to control my life. I want you to control my life." That is why unleashing unforgiveness can be unbelievable.

Remember my experience with the Doberman and the gas station bench? Last time we compared that scenario to our lives. We said we can be leashed to a bench full of people we have not forgiven. And instead of dealing with these relationships, we drag that bench behind us into every other situation in our lives. The result can be a life full of collateral damage.

Who is sitting on your bench? Maybe it's an ex-spouse, a parent, a teacher, an uncle, or a coach. Who are you dragging around from relationship to relationship?

Could it be that you're pointing the finger at the wrong person? Could it be that you need to point the finger at yourself for keeping that leash connected to the bench? Maybe you're dragging the bench into your relationships and you're causing collateral damage. If you will let God untie your leash from that bench of unforgiveness it will be unbelievable!

EMOTIONALLY

The first unbelievable benefit is the emotional benefit that occurs when we allow God to unleash our unforgiveness. God has feelings, too. And being made in the image of God, we are emotional creatures. But when we allow unforgiveness to reign, our emotions can get out of whack.

Resentment kills a fool.... Job 5:2

The word resentment means to feel again. It means to rehearse something over and over in our minds. And the more we replay that situation in our minds, the more our emotions become whacked and the more miserable we become. When

I become miserable, I have a tendency to make others around me miserable. When I'm feeling negative, I want you to feel negative, too. That's the way we are. Hurt people hurt people. (Y)-b

2. How has a damaged relationship wreaked havoc on your emotions?

_____

_____

_____

_____

Unforgiveness can eat our emotions alive. It can cause us to become negative. But when you encounter negativity in others, I challenge you to look beyond the what and look to1 the why. It could be that they've never experienced the forgiveness of God. And because of that, negativity plays a huge role in their lives.

3. How have you seen someone's hurt from one relationship damage other relationships? (Y)-c

_____

_____

_____

_____

Have you noticed the technological advances of cell phones? The newest versions are smaller, lighter and filled with cool new features. It's not hard to find a cell phone that is on the leading edge of technology. I've discovered something about technology, though. Technology over promises and under delivers.

One Sunday morning I was pulling out of my driveway at about 7:30 am. I usually call my brother Ben before I speak to the church just to talk or we might have a prayer together. This particular morning, I tried to call my brother twelve times and never got through. Technology over promises, but it under delivers. It has limitations.

Unforgiveness is the same way. It over promises and under delivers. You might think resentment works, but it will always under deliver. I have never seen a commercial that says, "Resentment will refresh your spirit." That's not going to happen because resentment will not get you where you want to go. When we take a step of faith and allow God to unleash unforgiveness, though, he will release us from some incredible emotional pain.

RELATIONALLY

Another unbelievable benefit of unleashing unforgiveness is the relational benefit.

> *Get rid of all bitterness, rage and anger, brawling and slander, along with every form of malice. Be kind and compassionate to one another, forgiving each other, just as in Christ God forgave you. Ephesians 4:31-32*

That verse is challenging to me as a married man, as a father, as a pastor, and as just a human being. I should live a life of forgiveness that causes me to forgive others before they even do their part. I should forgive others even if they never do their part.

Jesus was involved in preemptive forgiveness. In other words, Jesus did his part before we even thought about doing our part. Jesus took the initiative. He died on the cross for all of our sins and rose again long before we ever turned from our sins, before we ever looked to him. And because of that, we should do some preemptive forgiving.

4. How do you think forgiving a person before they even ask for forgiveness could help mend that relationship quicker?

_____

_____

_____

_____

5. How could practicing preemptive forgiveness be healthier for you than waiting for the person to ask for forgiveness?

_____

_____

_____

_____

A lot of people think they can't forgive until they feel like it. Ninety-nine percent of the time I don't _feel_ like forgiving. I don't _feel_ like releasing the person. I don't _feel_ like canceling the debt. I think, "If I did that, I would minimize what they said about me."

But that's simply not true. Forgiving is not minimizing the hurt and the pain. It's cancelling a debt because of the debt you have been forgiven by God. The situation may still exist, but the debt is cancelled.

Here is something about unforgiveness that you probably have not thought about: Unforgiveness, like love, can bind people together. Let's say you're a divorced woman or man whose ex committed multiple affairs on you. Let's say you're still leashed up to them for the horrible way they treated you. They are on the bench and you're dragging them around from relationship to relationship. To release them, to drop them, to forgive them would mean to lose your last connection with them. Hate, maybe, has become your hobby. The problem is that hate and resentment have consumed your emotions. And you don't want God to come in and untie the leash from the bench because it will break your relationship. It will sever the final tie with that person, and you aren't ready to do that.

When you allow that to happen, you end up missing out on some amazing relational blessings God wants to give you. God wants to free you up from the pain and frustration of failed relationships and lead you to safety. If you'll just trust him and allow him the opportunity to do it, you'll discover that unleashing unforgiveness is truly unbelievable.

Here's something else about doing the preemptive work of forgiveness. It's not a one-way street. Yes, we've got to forgive those who have hurt us. But we are also called to do take the initiative with the people we've wronged. We need to ask for forgiveness from those people we have hurt, damaged and messed around.

6. In general, asking for forgiveness is never as bad as we imagine it will be. Why do you think we fear a strong reaction when we ask for forgiveness? (Y)-d

_____

_____

_____

_____

I was thinking about the process of asking for forgiveness, and I realized something we all have a tendency to do. Just saying, "I'm sorry," is pitiful. That's not forgiveness work. When all I say is "Sorry," I'm still in control. Or we'll say, "If you took what I said wrong, I'm sorry. I apologize if I hurt you in any way." That's not the real work of forgiveness.

Here's real forgiveness work. "I was wrong. _Will you forgive me?_" Now I've made myself vulnerable. That's what we should do when we ask for forgiveness. Don't worry if they refuse to forgive you. Biblically speaking, you've done your part. But don't forget to take that situation to God and ask that other person, "_Will you forgive me?_"

7. Practice apologizing in advance. It's a good idea to work out your conversation ahead of time. Tell the group what you might say if you were apologizing for hurting someone and let the group give you feedback. Let them tell you what they liked and disliked about your apology.

_____

_____

_____

_____

Even though it's important to be proactive with those we have hurt, it is impossible to track down everybody you've ever hurt in the past. If you have questions as far as who you should go to for forgiveness, when you should do it or other concerns, seek Christian counseling or talk to a trusted Christian friend.

Everybody should be in the forgiving business. We need to do our part in the reconciliation, our part in offering forgiveness and also our part in releasing the person who has hurt us. Unbelievable things will happen in the relational realm when we unleash unforgiveness. Ⓨ-**e**

PHYSICALLY

There's a physical benefit to forgiveness as well. A little paper cut can be a dangerous wound. Although it starts small, it can become infected and poison your system if it is not taken care of properly.

The same is true with unforgiveness. A little bit of unforgiveness can poison my entire system. As you read in the first lesson, for two years I harbored bitterness, resentment and revenge. I struggled with unforgiveness in a real way. I've also been leashed up to a coach that messed me around. I'm telling you that harboring these poisonous feeling does not work. It can poison your entire system. It can poison the greatness that God has for your life.

A heart at peace gives life to the body.... Proverbs 14:30

8. Admit to any of the following that applies to you. Because of unforgiveness, have you ever:

- **Lost sleep?**
- **Felt sick to your stomach?**
- **Worried to the point of a headache?**
- **Experienced anxiety about being around someone?**

Science is just now discovering what the Bible has said for thousands of years: unleashing unforgiveness can benefit you physically. A recent study showed that giving up grudges can reduce chronic back pain. Another study found that forgiveness limited relapses among women battling substance abuse problems. An even more intriguing project explored how just *thinking* about empathy and reconciliation sparks activity in the brain's left middle temporal gyrus, suggesting we all have a mental forgiveness center just waiting to be tapped.

One study at Stanford University made sure to emphasize that forgiving doesn't mean condoning the offense. God is not saying when we release someone we have to become best buddies with them. You still might not have this great vibe with the person in question. But we are called to do our part in reconciliation. This Stanford study also stated that letting go of a grudge can slash one's stress level by up to 50 percent!

Volunteers of that study have shown improvements in energy, mood, sleep quality, and overall physical vitality. The doctor in charge of the project is quoted as saying, "Carrying around a load of bitterness and anger at how unfairly you were treated is very, very toxic."

Do you see the brilliance of God? Do you see the love of God? He does not want us to live life chained and leashed up to unforgiveness. He knows that unleashing unforgiveness is unbelievable.

SPIRITUALLY

Unleashing unforgiveness is unbelievable emotionally, relationally and physically. And it is unbelievable spiritually as well.

> *And when you stand praying, if you hold anything against anyone, forgive him, so that your Father in heaven may forgive you your sins. Mark 11:25*

If we hold on to our unforgiveness, we will reap the consequences. If we hold grudges, refusing to forgive those who have messed us around, our connection with God is going to be damaged.

That's a tall order for a self-centered person like me. Supernaturally, though, God can unleash unforgiveness in you and me. Through Christ, I have the ability to walk in forgiveness and I can walk in freedom. This whole forgiveness issue starts with what God has done for me through Christ. And it should continue as I forgive others.

In Luke 19, Jesus met Zaccheus. The two of them shared the quintessential power lunch. Zaccheus was a guy that routinely ripped off his fellow countrymen. After his encounter with Jesus, Zaccheus was so ambushed and smitten by the forgiveness of God that he walked out on his beautiful porch and said this, "Here and now I give half of my possessions to the poor. And if I have cheated anybody out of anything, I will pay back four times the amount" (Luke 19:8). When Zaccheus experienced the forgiving power of God, it impacted everything in his life. He understood that unleashing unforgiveness is unbelievable. Ⓨ-f

9. What could you do as a Zaccheus-like response to God's forgiveness?

_____

_____

_____

_____

> *If you forgive anyone, I also forgive him. And what I have forgiven—if there was anything to forgive—I have forgiven in the sight of Christ for your sake, in order that Satan might not outwit us. For we are not unaware of his schemes. 2 Corinthians 2:10-11*

As believers, we have to realize what the evil one is up to. The evil one wants to use unforgiveness to mess us up. So every time we are tempted to harbor a hurt, to place someone on our bench, to get leashed up to unforgiveness, we've got to say, "Hey, evil one, I know what you're up to! You're trying to mess me around."

10. How could you combat the strategies Satan uses to prevent you from offering and receiving the forgiveness of God?

_____

_____

_____

_____

WRAP IT UP

I know that many of you are tethered to a bench of unforgiveness. Some of us may be dragging around four or five park benches with loads and loads of people from our past who we have not forgiven. When we do this we are forfeiting the unbelievable things God wants to do in our lives. I know you might not feel like it and most of the time; I don't either. But when we use God's grace and mercy to help us unleash our unforgiveness, we will discover some unbelievable results!

Prayer Requests:

_____

_____

_____

_____

_____

_____

_____

_____

_____

_____

_____

_____

_____

Notes:

_____

_____

_____

_____

_____

_____

_____

_____

_____

_____

_____

_____

_____

_____

_____

_____

_____

_____

_____

STEP IT UP

Take a step further over the next few days and spend some time reflecting on the following devotional thoughts that reinforce the previous session. Use these as reminders to take what you've learned and apply it to your everyday life.

DAY 1

Job 5:2

Americans spend millions of dollars each year on methods to improve their emotional health. There are support groups, counseling, medicine and nontraditional techniques all designed to help you achieve healthier emotions. The importance of emotional health is becoming a topic of great prominence and importance in our culture. God is probably wondering what took our culture so long.

God understands the intricate details of who we are because he created us. He knows exactly what will happen physically, mentally and spiritually when our emotions are unhealthy. He also knows that unforgiveness causes us numerous problems. God has given us clear instructions for dealing with our emotions, especially when it comes to unforgiveness. When we do not follow God's clear instructions, we are being foolish. How else would you describe the creature turning his back on his Creator? The Bible calls anyone who ignores the God's instructions as foolish, especially in the book of Proverbs. If we are foolish enough to ignore God's wisdom for our lives, it can hurt and even destroy us.

Emotional destruction is not limited to "emotional" people. Even the reserved, steady personalities struggle with emotional health. Everyone has emotions and lives in a world marred by sin, so everyone is vulnerable to emotional problems. God's principles for living will enable you to navigate through the hard times we all face.

How have you experienced unforgiveness affecting your emotions?

Ask God to give you emotional health by helping you overcome areas unforgiveness.

Notes:

_____

_____

_____

_____

_____

_____

_____

_____

Prayer Requests:

_____

_____

_____

_____

_____

_____

_____

_____

_____

_____

_____

DAY 2

Ephesians 4:31-32

Unforgiveness can be a relationship killer. It will not only destroy the relationships in which there is unforgiveness festering, but also it will destroy future relationships. If you are carrying around bitterness, rage and anger in one relationship, it will carry over to other relationships that you don't even consider. The bitterness of one relationship can inadvertently poison other relationships.

Think about someone you consider to be a bitter person. Chances are, they have vented some of those bitter feelings at you. And the more deeply this person is hurt, the more you will experience those feelings of bitterness. The result of unforgiveness is toxic relationships that trickle out to each person connected to the one who is hurt.

For the health of all your relationships, give yourself a gift. If you are still leashed to unforgiveness, release those people on the bench you are dragging around. Do it for your own health and the health of all your relationships. You can't keep the toxins of unforgiveness limited to just one relationship. Get rid of them before you poison the people around you.

Ask God to show you if you are carrying around unforgiveness to other relationships.

If God shows you any areas that are being poisoned, ask for his healing in all your relationships.

Notes:

_____

_____

_____

_____

_____

_____

_____

_____

Prayer Requests:

_____

_____

_____

_____

_____

_____

_____

_____

_____

_____

DAY 3

Proverbs 14:30

Have you ever wrestled with an issue in your heart for an extended period of time? The battle can drain you. It can leave you feeling as if you had been in an actual wrestling match. However, it is extremely rewarding when we resolve a difficult issue. We often regain that lost sense of peace in our hearts. And our bodies respond differently when the issue is resolved. In those moments, you can probably relate to today's verse. It is as if you have been given life.

Jesus came so we could have abundant life (John 10:10). That applies to more than just our spiritual life. God created our physical body and knows exactly what it needs to run at its full potential. Unleashing unforgiveness is a way to open our bodies to the health God desires. And that includes an abundant physical life.

The process of gaining physical health from forgiveness is similar to the process of gaining physical health from diet and exercise. It is just that… a process. When you begin to forgive those you have held grudges against, you will begin to see the benefits of those difficult decisions. You will experience rapid moments of growth along with slower moments of building. If you persist in the process you will reach a point where your body is functioning the way God desires. You will have an abundant life that is free from unforgiveness. You will have the health that comes from a heart at peace.

Ask God to show you any areas you are still struggling with unforgiveness. Then, ask him to show you what you need to do to begin the healing.

Notes:

_____

_____

_____

_____

_____

_____

_____

_____

Prayer Requests:

_____

_____

_____

_____

_____

_____

_____

_____

_____

_____

_____

_____

DAY 4

2 Corinthians 2:10-11

Did you catch that last part? Satan is scheming. He is devising plans to hinder your relationship with God. He is placing obstacles in your relationships with others. He is setting snares in your inner thoughts. He wants to take you down. He is fully committed to your downfall and he will use whatever weapon he can.

Unforgiveness is part of Satan's schemes. You may think by holding on to that resentment or bitterness you are in control of the situation, but in reality, you are handing it off. You are putting the person who hurt you in control. You are giving them power in your life. By doing this, you are ultimately relinquishing control to Satan who is celebrating your resentment and bitterness. Satan is applauding your moves to hand the leash of your life to others. That gives him opportunities for manipulation and control of your life.

Have you ever thought of it that way? Did you realize you were empowering Satan every time you stayed leashed to unforgiveness? That is a scary thought. Yesterday you were reminded that Jesus came to give abundant life. There is another part to that verse. The same verse tells us that Satan comes to steal, kill and destroy (John 10:10). If you stay leashed up to unforgiveness, you will succumb to the destruction of Satan.

How does staying leashed to unforgiveness empower the person you have not forgiven?

How does unforgiveness give Satan power in your life?

Notes:

_____

_____

_____

_____

_____

_____

_____

_____

Prayer Requests:

_____

_____

_____

_____

_____

_____

_____

_____

_____

_____

_____

DAY 5

Proverbs 19:11

Unleashing unforgiveness is unbelievable. Today you read how it is to your benefit to overlook an offense. The idea behind the word "overlook" is that you pass by that offense. It is not that you do not notice when someone has wronged you. Overlooking a wrong can only happen when we're aware of something against us. To honor God, he will ask you to overlook those wrongs against you. You will be able to get passed the offense and get on with your life. And you'll save a lot of time if you don't climb into the pit of unforgiveness.

It is to your glory to pass beyond the offense. Christ proved this. By not becoming bogged down by the wrongs committed against him, he was able to accomplish his purpose of salvation for all of us. He was slandered, beaten and humiliated, yet he moved on. He kept going for the glory that awaited him. He offers glory to those of us who gain their strength from God, allowing him to heal and execute his flawless justice.

Take time to consider a time when you were able to forgive someone. What benefits did you receive from this experience? Ask God to help you store those in your heart for the next time someone offends you.

FORGIVENESS FORGIVE FOR GOOD

Notes:

_____

_____

_____

_____

_____

_____

_____

_____

Prayer Requests:

_____

_____

_____

_____

_____

_____

_____

_____

_____

_____

BUILD A BRIDGE AND GET OVER IT

START IT UP

Have you ever tripped in public, embarrassing and hurting yourself at the same time? You are filled with a myriad of emotions. You want to laugh, hide and soothe your pain. Chances are good that you've tripped and fallen in public. It's embarrassing and it can hurt.

1. What are some funny or embarrassing things you've experienced?

_____

_____

_____

_____

In time, those embarrassing moments can turn to laughter. The cuts and bruises heal, your ego heals, and you can usually laugh it off at some point. Unforgiveness, though, is a way we hurt ourselves that doesn't heal on its own. We have to make a decision to unleash our unforgiveness, or it will always be an open wound.

TALK IT UP

When I harbor hurt, when I hold tight to resentment, anger or unforgiveness, I'm giving the leash in my life to people who've hurt me. I'm saying, "You control my life. You run the show." And when I give someone else control of my life, I hinder what God wants for me. I end up forfeiting the amazing freedom that comes from unleashing unforgivness.

UNLEASHING UNFORGIVENESS IS UNDENIABLE

But if you do not forgive men their sins, your Father will not forgive your sins. Matthew 6:15

In other words, if I'm not right with the people in my life, why should God forgive me? Why should God grant me vertical forgiveness if I'm not giving horizontal forgiveness? As a believer, I've been greatly forgiven. I'm a sinner. I'm a moral foul up. And so are you. And yet, our gracious God has done the work of forgiveness. Because of that, I have a responsibility to forgive others.

When you choose not to forgive others, you are telling God you do not agree with his plan. You are telling God you think your way is better. We need to remember that the only reason we have a relationship with God is because he forgave us of our funk and our junk. When we readily accept God's forgiveness but deny that same kind of forgiveness to others, we are being hypocrites. Doing the work of forgiveness is critical to living like Christ. When we refuse to offer forgiveness, we hurt our relationship with God and miss out on his best for our lives. Ⓨ-a

2. Share an example of how your own anger and resentment towards another person hurt your relationship with God.

_____

_____

_____

_____

We all need to defer to God, to give him our life. If we don't live this forgiveness thing out, whether we've hurt the person or they've hurt us, then we're going to break our fellowship with God. And we're going to miss out on the undeniable benefits of his forgiveness in our everyday lives. There are several ways unforgiveness hinders us from experiencing what God has for us.

UNFORGIVENESS HINDERS OUR GENEROSITY

Unforgiveness also hinders away the generosity that God wants me to have. I become a selfish person when I harbor unforgiveness. Whenever you hurt me and I forgive you for your actions, I'm giving a gift that will help both of us. If I hurt you and ask for your forgiveness, I'm also giving something. In both cases, I'm being generous.

In the first week we talked about the barriers to forgiveness—self-deception, self-defense, self-image and self-protection. All of these are centered on self. And selfish people, unforgiving people, are not generous people.

3. How is holding a grudge or not asking for forgiveness a selfish act?

_____

_____

_____

_____

When we forgive, we're being generous. And the person who benefits the most you're your forgiveness is you. Isn't that something? It's supernatural. You show me someone who is selfish and I'll show you someone who's never experienced the forgiveness of God. They might have intellectually received it, but they've not experienced it in the depth of their soul. Because they've not experienced it, they can't share it with others.

UNFORGIVENESS HINDERS OUR LOVE

Being leashed up to unforgiveness will also minimize the love I should have for other people. The Bible says that God is love. Because God loves me and he's given me this love, I should love others. Part of expressing love is forgiving others.

Therefore, as God's chosen people, holy and dearly loved, clothe yourselves with compassion, kindness, humility, gentleness and patience. Bear with each other and forgive whatever grievances you may have against one another. Forgive as the Lord forgave you. And over all these virtues put on love, which binds them all together in perfect unity. Colossians 3:12-14

If you are holding a grudge, it can prohibit you from loving others. Every time you are struggling with unforgiveness, it is difficult to love that person as you love yourself. Unforgiveness can prevent you from loving, but love can also be the key to overcoming your grudge. Ⓨ-b

4. How could love help you overcome your grudge and help you become compassionate, kind, humble, gentle, patient and forgiving?

Instead of asking, "How could they do this to me?" We should be asking, "Why am I doing this to myself?" Instead of saying, "Well, they hurt me. They took advantage of me. I can't believe they did this to me." We should be saying, "Why am I still leashed up to all this junk?"

Here's what I've discovered about my own life when I harbor a hurt: I like to share my hurts with others. I like to play the victim. I tell all my friends, "Can you believe what they did to me? Can you believe what they said about me? Can you believe this?"

I rehearse it over and over until finally I can tell my friends are thinking, "Ed, chill. Just shut up about all that stuff."

Attorneys have something called billable hours. As they build a case, they bill you per hour. We do the same thing in our lives when people hurt us. We build a case against our ex, our former best friend, or that person that totally messed us around in the business deal. And the currency we use to pay for the billable hours is an emotional currency. It zaps our energy. And it keeps us tethered to unforgiveness, messing up the way we think and act.

5. How has holding onto unforgiveness emotionally drained you?

The Bible says that when we are involved in unforgiveness, we are not only putting the leash in the hands of those who hurt us; we are also putting the leash in the devil's hands. That can be shocking and scary at the same time. You are giving the devil control when you stay tethered to unforgiveness.

> *"In your anger do not sin": Do not let the sun go down while you are still angry.... Ephesians 4:26-27*

There is this image of Christ-followers being passive, detached people who never experience anger or jealousy or any other of the so-called "negative emotions." If these soft Christians lose someone they love, they just smile because of the joy inside. If someone messes them around, they just grin in contentment. That is often the image, but is it honest? Is it real?

Here is a big question for believers. Is it a sin to be angry?

No! God gets angry. And as Christ-followers, we should get angry. We should get angry at injustice and at other sins that grieve the heart of God. It is a sin, though, when my anger gets the best of me. When I act out in my anger in a way that is opposite of Christ, then I am sinning.

6. In the following ways, how could you respond in anger without sinning? Ⓨ-c

- **An organization takes advantage of helpless people.**
- **Your friend is injured by a negligent driver.**
- **A co-worker spreads lies about you at work.**

So once again, being angry is not a sin. You sin when your anger gets the best of you, fueling these feelings and these words into actions that make you unlike Christ. So the Bible says, "In your anger, do not sin." If I allow anger to get a foothold in my life, that is a sin. If I allow anger to boil up in my life, that is a sin. If I store up my anger and hurt only to use it to hurt someone later, that is a sin.

Too many of us have forgotten the real source of our anger. We've forgotten that it's all about that original act that hasn't been forgiven. Instead of dealing with that one act, we transfer it to our spouse, or coworker or child. The source of our anger could be something 10 or 20 years in the past! Imagine all the collateral damage you are causing because you haven't dealt with that original act.

The last part of that verse says, *"...do not let the sun go down while you're still angry...."*

If we allow the sun to set too many times on our unforgiveness, anger and resentment, then we forget the source of it. We forget where the leash is connected. We don't know the source of our unforgiveness, so we try to change environments. "I'll just move from this marriage to that marriage. I'll go from that friendship to this friendship, from this partnership to that partnership." But we cause all kinds of collateral damage when we ignore the source of our bitterness.

7. How have you seen unresolved anger dragged from one relationship to the next?

_____

_____

_____

_____

For so many of us, the sun has set so much on our anger, resentment and unforgiveness that we don't know the source of it anymore. Just changing environments does not work. That mentality would be like me driving home after work and getting into a wreck. Then the paramedics rush to the scene and say, "Ed, I want to help you with your injuries." But, instead of dealing with my injury I just tell them, "Don't touch me. If you'll just take me to another place; if you'll just get me away from the crash site, my injuries will be okay."

That would be ridiculous, but we have all done that with unforgiveness. We say, "Well yeah, they hurt me, but if you'll just change my environment I'll be okay." But are we really okay?

This passage continues. It further explains how we are putting the leash of unforgiveness in the devil's hands.

...and do not give the devil a foothold. Ephesians 4:27

I would argue that unforgiveness is the biggest obstacle that keeps Christians from experiencing the freedom that God desires. If I'm Satan, I'm going to try to infiltrate believers' lives and mess them around with this unforgiveness thing. Satan tries to get a foothold, and if we give it to him, he'll take a stronghold on your life. A stronghold is a base of enemy operations. From the stronghold, he can easily put us in a chokehold.

8. How have you seen Satan take a small situation and wreak havoc on an entire life?

_____

_____

_____

_____

It shouldn't be that way. Life is too short to live that way. Unforgiveness will burn up our lives and we'll miss the best God has for us. Knowing that should lead us to untie our leash and follow God's motivators for forgiveness.

MOTIVATIONS FOR FORGIVENESS

Bear with each other and forgive whatever grievances you may have against one another. Forgive as the Lord forgave you. Colossians 3:13

Against the backdrop of Colossians 3:13, there are three motivators for forgiveness. As believers, we need to think about these three things that will motivate us to release someone from their actions, or to ask forgiveness for our own actions.

Number one, we need to *consider the cross*. Consider what Jesus Christ has done on the cross for you. Consider the preemptive forgiveness that he did before you even asked for it. That should motivate all of us to do the work of forgiveness. Ⓨ-d

9. What are a few things that could remind you to consider the cross when you are dealing with unforgiveness?

_____

_____

_____

_____

Here's a second motivator. _Realize that resentment does not work._ It will not get you where you want to go. You will not get back at the person. Think about this. The person who hurt you probably doesn't even realize they've hurt you. And even if they know, they're out having a good time and while you are in the corner licking your wounds.

10. What has helped you deal with resentment in your own life?

_____

_____

_____

_____

The third reason that we should be motivated to do the forgiveness work is because _we all need an infusion of forgiveness in the future._ I know I'm going to sin in the future. Hopefully, I will not sin as much in the future as I have in the past, but I'm going to sin. I need forgiveness. I need grace. I need mercy. And you do, too. That should motivate me to release someone else when they need forgiveness.

We have talked in-depth about needing to unleash unforgiveness. But we have only been general about who we forgive. Let's get more specific and look at three main groups of people we should forgive.

BIG 3 OF FORGIVENESS

The first group we need to forgive is the _people we love the most_: spouses, parents, close friends. Forgiveness should be the most natural with this group since you care about them the most.

The second group is *those in authority over us*. It could be teachers, supervisors, coaches, government employees or more.

The third of the big three are *those we are in competition with*. (Y)-e

Forgiving the people we are in competition with is often the most difficult group to forgive. I struggled with this for a long time. When I was in seminary, I started a basketball league. But I wasn't just the commissioner, I also played (That was a big mistake).

In one particular game, we were playing a team I really wanted to beat. But there the referees did not show up. I looked in the stands and saw this guy who looked like a basketball player so I walked up to him and I said, "Hey, would you mind reffing this game?" He agreed and I gave him the whistle.

The game started, and got out of hand quickly. Elbows and arguments were flying. My brother Ben played on my team. On one play, he went up for a shot and got slammed to the floor. At that point I had enough. I walked up to this substitute referee and got in his face. I didn't yell at him, but I said, "Give me your whistle. You don't know up from down about basketball. Get off the court and go back to the stands!"

The guy didn't sit back down in the stands. He walked out of the gym in disgust. I just thought, "Well, he deserved that. When we're in the heat of competition that's just the way it is."

After the game I completely forgot about the situation. But as I tried to pray over the next few days, my prayers fell like air balls. I knew I was in the wrong. I had sinned against this guy. But I tried to justify it by telling God, "I can't track the guy down now. I have no idea where he is. Besides, he messed up. Someone was going to get hurt, so I had to do what I did."

11. What are excuses you have made to try to get out of asking for forgiveness?

_____

_____

_____

_____

Finally, I was broken by the grace and mercy of God. I realized the extent to which I had been forgiven by God, and I knew what I had to do. It took me two days, but I finally tracked the guy down. I called him and made an appointment with him for the next day. As I walked into his office, I was so scared that I was shaking. Then I looked at him and said the four most difficult words in the human language, *"Will you forgive me?"*

To my amazement he looked at me and said, "Yes."

And that was it. As I left the meeting, he was still hurt. But I did the work that God wanted me to do. And when I left, I had to trust that God would take care of him. God had already worked in my own life; I knew that he would work in this man's life, too.

Most people have been caught in the moment of competition. It does not have to be on the court or field of athletics. The competition could be in the classroom, the boardroom, the living room or anywhere else. In those moments, we can get so overworked that we do or say the wrong thing. Those are the opportunities that we have no option but to do the work of forgiveness—asking or giving.

12. In times of competition, what has helped you keep from losing your cool in the heat of the moment?

_____

_____

_____

_____

WRAP IT UP

God can teach us life-changing lessons when it comes to unleashing unforgiveness. Don't let a place of unforgiveness hinder you any longer. Build a bridge of forgiveness and get over it. Unleash your unforgiveness so you can experience the unbelievable benefits God has for you!

Prayer Requests:

_____

_____

_____

_____

_____

_____

_____

Notes:

_____

_____

_____

_____

_____

_____

_____

_____

_____

_____

_____

_____

_____

STEP IT UP

Take a step further over the next few days and spend some time reflecting on the following devotional thoughts that reinforce the previous session. Use these as reminders to take what you've learned and apply it to your everyday life.

DAY 1

Colossians 3:12

We need a closet check! Does your wardrobe match that of Colossians 3:12? We should clothe ourselves with compassion, kindness, humility, gentleness and patience. Do you wrap your life in those things? Those characteristics should stand out to those who are around you as if you showed up in full length fur coat on a summer day. When we are clothed in the qualities of Christ, we will stand out from the world.

All of those characteristics apply to forgiveness. If you have compassion, you care about others. You are not just out for yourself. And, it is a lot easier to forgive those you care about. If kindness and gentleness are part of your nature, you will be less likely to struggle with forgiveness. Humility goes a long way as well. A humble person remembers how often they have needed forgiveness, compelling them to make their relationships right. With patience in the mix, you will take time to understand the other person. This helps you look past an offense because you took time to look at the situation with more objectivity. A person clothed in these characteristics is well equipped to unleash unforgiveness.

How does your wardrobe stack up? Are you struggling with compassion, kindness, humility, gentleness or patience?

FORGIVENESS

Notes:

_____

_____

_____

_____

_____

_____

_____

_____

Prayer Requests:

_____

_____

_____

_____

_____

_____

_____

_____

_____

_____

DAY 2

Colossians 3:13-14

"Forgive as the Lord forgave you" is a powerful thought. That is no small task. It requires you to think about how God forgave you. He did not make you jump through a bunch of hoops to receive his offer of forgiveness. God could have required any number of things, yet he made it easy to obtain it. God does not put a time limit on the offer of his forgiveness. He does not offer it for two days, two weeks or two years. His offer is good for all of our lives, even on our deathbed.

God's forgiveness is not limited. He does not give us a limit on the amount of times he will forgive us, even when it is for the same offense. His forgiveness is also unlimited in that it is for everyone. You do not have to be a person of prominence to experience the forgiveness of God. God does not forgive on a short-term basis. He will not bring up the offense later on. God forgives and chooses to remember our sins no more.

"Forgive as the Lord forgave you." It is a daunting task, but empowered by the God who set the standard, we are able to forgive on such a high level.

How does your forgiveness compare to God's forgiveness?

Notes:

_____

_____

_____

_____

_____

_____

_____

_____

Prayer Requests:

_____

_____

_____

_____

_____

_____

_____

_____

_____

_____

DAY 3

Ephesians 4:26

Do you remember the superhero Flash? He was known for his amazing speed. Like most comic book heroes, he gained his supernatural ability out of adversity. Flash turned his adversity into an advantage. The result is an amazing hero with lightning quick abilities.

We could all use a little Flash when it comes to forgiveness. We need to learn from the adversities of our past, and develop the ability to forgive in a flash. Lightning quick forgiveness is a biblical thing. The Bible described it as not letting the sun go down on our anger. That is not easy even for those experienced in the work of forgiveness. It takes work to deal with the issues as they happen. And it takes commitment to follow through with the solutions instead of procrastinating.

Not dealing with an issue is like having an open wound. The longer you wait to treat it, the greater the risk for infection. If infection happens, you will have a harder time healing than if you had just dealt with it quickly in the beginning. Forgiveness wounds get infected when we let the original issue fester in our minds. When we let our wounds turn on the rotisserie grill of our minds, we will make the situation much worse. The result is a new set of problems for unleashing unforgiveness that never existed in the first place.

On a scale of one to ten with ten being "flash fast," how fast do you forgive?

What keeps you from forgiving more quickly?

FORGIVENESS

Notes:

_____

_____

_____

_____

_____

_____

_____

_____

Prayer Requests:

_____

_____

_____

_____

_____

_____

_____

_____

_____

_____

_____

DAY 4

Ecclesiastes 7:21-22

"You're asking for it." Have you ever had someone tell you that? It is generally a warning that you are doing something that will lead to trouble. Unfortunately we are probably knowingly or unknowingly "asking for" a lot of the trouble in our lives. Most of the trouble we face is directly related to the decisions we make. That is why we react harshly when we encounter trouble we did not deserve.

When it comes to unforgiveness issues, many are asking for it. That is the point of the verses you read in Ecclesiastes. The warning is to avoid getting involved in all the things that people talk about. If you live your life in the middle of everyone else's business, you are going to find out things you don't like. These things might even offend you. If you are involved in everyone else's business, you are asking for trouble.

The other part of this verse is that you are asking for it when you do not allow others the same leeway you need. In the Ecclesiastes example, the master should not be offended when the servant says something in anger about him because he has probably committed the same offense towards those over him. The principle is that we should remember to extend the grace we need to others. This would stop many offenses from ever becoming an unforgiveness issue.

When it comes to unforgiveness, are you asking for it?

FORGIVENESS

Notes:

_____

_____

_____

_____

_____

_____

_____

_____

_____

Prayer Requests:

_____

_____

_____

_____

_____

_____

_____

_____

_____

_____

_____

DAY 5

Proverbs 25:21-22

Have you ever had the desire to get someone back for messing you around? Have you ever dreamed about just the right thing to get someone back? Sometimes you might imagine saying just the right comeback to squash your enemy. Maybe the perfect comeback is giving them a taste of their own medicine... except a double dose. The perfect payback could be in the form of a courtroom. There really are lots of options.

The next time you want to get somebody back, try this. When they do something wrong to you, serve them. Try a "no holds barred" act of kindness. Find out something they need and provide for them. Man, that'll teach 'em!

That might not be your first thought, but that is God's plan for payback. God's payback plan is not an easy road for the offender. You might be serving, but that person will experience the frustration of having the offense negated. God's dream is to turn your enemy into a friend through your kindness. Even if that does not happen, you will have at least shown them God's noble character. That display of character has its own reward.

Not only will your act punish those who offended you, but also it will earn you a reward. Handling offenses in the right way is an opportunity to earn God's blessing. When you look at from that angle, it brings being offended into a new light.

The next time someone offends you, pay them back. Get them real good! Give them a double dose! Just make sure you follow God's plan for payback.

FORGIVENESS

Notes:

_____

_____

_____

_____

_____

_____

_____

_____

_____

Prayer Requests:

_____

_____

_____

_____

_____

_____

_____

_____

_____

_____

4-D FORGIVENESS

FORGIVENESS

START IT UP

Several years ago I was in the middle of a sermon and two ladies sitting towards the front of the auditorium got up and slowly walked out of the room. As a speaker, that is one of the most distracting things that anyone can do. If it's an emergency, that's one thing. But to me, that incident was just too much to take.

As these ladies walked out of this facility, I stopped my sermon, looked directly at them and said, "Ladies, I'm getting ready to read Psalm 105:13. You might want to memorize that verse as you're leaving church early!" Everybody started laughing, but I was totally out of line. I was wrong. I sinned. After the service, I tried to justify what I'd done, but I knew I was wrong.

That afternoon I talked to my wife about it and she really let me know that I was out of line. The problem now was finding these two ladies. I had no idea who they were or where they were. I remember thinking, "How can I possibly find them? They'll probably never come back to church. I blew it. I messed up." Since I didn't know how to track them down, I took a bold step and apologized to the entire church before the next week's sermon.

The following day, I got a note in my office from the ladies: "Dear Ed, we are so sorry that we disrupted the service that day, and we accept your apology." Not only did they write that note, but they sent it along with a delicious dish of lasagna!

1. Tell some of your forgiveness stories. What were some of your most memorable times asking for forgiveness?

_____

_____

_____

_____

TALK IT UP

Throughout this study we've been talking about the real F-word—forgiveness. During this session, we are going to see that forgiveness is really a futuristic thing. And for our future to flourish through forgiveness, we've got to make peace with our past.

In week one, we learned that unleashing unforgiveness is _unnatural_. We said there's something in all of us that likes to be leashed up to unforgiveness. When someone messes me around, hurts me, or takes advantage of me, I want to get them back. I want to make them pay. I want to seek that sweet revenge.

During week two, we learned that unleashing unforgiveness is _unbelievable_. God wants us to unleash the unforgiveness in your live because he wants you to discover the unbelievable benefits. The upside for forgiveness is monstrous—emotionally, relationally, physically and spiritually.

This week, we discover the third thing about unleashing unforgiveness.

UNLEASHING UNFORGIVENESS IS UNENDING

Most of the time we think about three dimensions: height, width and depth. The fourth dimension is that supernatural dimension, the dimension that God wants us to walk in. We can only do this forgiveness work when we live our lives in the fourth dimension. When we reside there, we discover that unleashing unforgiveness is unending.

God tells us that Christ-followers should live in a constant state of forgiveness. That's something that I cannot do naturally, but it is possible in the fourth dimension.

There are always new facets of unleashing unforgiveness that we will discover when we live our lives in the fourth dimension. There is always something more we should be doing. Unleashing unforgiveness is unending.

2. How many times a month should you either have to forgive someone or ask for forgiveness? (Y)-a

_____

_____

_____

_____

You might be wondering, "What do I need to do when it comes to unleashing unforgiveness? How can I do the work of forgiveness?"

You need to live in the 4-D land of forgiveness, the fourth dimension. There are four things that all of us need to do starting today. And it all emerges from the grace and the mercy of God.

DEFER TO GOD

The first thing we need to do is *defer to God*. Simply admit to him, "God, this whole forgiveness thing is from you. I've been greatly forgiven. Because I've been greatly forgiven, I want to greatly forgive others. God, I want to live on the final frontier of forgiveness."

> *And with that he breathed on them and said, "Receive the Holy Spirit. If you forgive anyone his sins, they are forgiven; if you do not forgive them, they are not forgiven." John 20:22-23*

Here's the context. Jesus had just risen from the dead. The disciples were locked in a little room, scared to death. Jesus walked in, and the Bible says in John 20:22, "He breathed on them and said, 'Receive the Holy Spirit.'"

What did he say next? Look at verse 23. He talked about forgiveness. "If you forgive anyone his sins, they are forgiven; if you do not forgive them, they are not forgiven."

Jesus had just done the work of forgiveness for all humanity on the cross. His resurrection was evidence of his perfectly righteous life and his perfect sacrifice for the sin of mankind. Then the Holy Spirit came upon the disciples and equipped them to do the work of forgiveness.

This whole thing has to be from God. We've got to defer to him. If you don't feel it or want it, tell God about it. He will give you the power and the octane to do the work. It's intrinsically woven into the very fabric and framework of who he is. So ask him for help and he will come through. Ⓨ-b

3. What have you done to turn to God for help when you were unleashing unforgiveness?

_____

_____

_____

_____

4. How has God helped you with unforgiveness?

_____

_____

_____

_____

DECIDE TO TAKE THE INITIATIVE

The second thing we've got to do is *decide to take the initiative*. God gives us the grace to do it, but we have the option to make a decision or not. The power is there, but we make the choice to activate it. Ⓨ-c

Do you remember the prodigal son? The prodigal son turned his back on his family and ran far away. When things got tough, he finally went back home to beg his father to let him come home. But he never had to beg, because the father took the initiative.

> ... while he (the prodigal son) was still a long way off, his father saw him and was filled with compassion for him; he ran to his son, threw his arms around him and kissed him. Luke 15:20

After all the boy had done, this father still took the initiative and welcomed him back home with open arms.

In the first lesson of this study we learned about a story Jesus told in which a king forgave his servant of a ten million dollar debt—a debt the servant had no chance of repaying. That king took the initiative to forgive the debt. What was Christ saying? Take the initiative to do the work of forgiveness.

5. How can you take the initiative when someone has wronged you?

_____

_____

_____

_____

We serve an initiative taking God. He is all about preemptive forgiveness. Jesus did the work on the cross. He did his part long before we even thought about doing our part. As Christ followers, that's what we're called to do.

> If it is possible, as far as it depends on you, live at peace with everyone. Romans 12:18

6. How does preemptive forgiveness (both in the sense of forgiving others and asking for forgiveness) relate to the verse you just read?

_____

_____

_____

FORGIVENESS

It's our choice. If we want to live at peace with others, it's our choice to ask for forgiveness when we have wronged someone. It's also our choice to forgive someone else, even if they have not asked for forgiveness. Like Christ, we should take the initiative.

DISENGAGE FROM YOUR EMOTIONS

I don't feel like forgiving people who hurt me. Do you? I just don't *feel* like it. I don't like people who hurt me. I'm mad at them. But that should not stop me from doing what God has told me to do. I didn't feel like going in front of the entire church and apologizing to those two women. But, I couldn't wait until I felt like it. If we wait until we feel like forgiving, then we'll never forgive.

We've got to live on the other side of our feelings. Feelings are freaky and fickle. We can't trust our feelings all the time. There are times I don't feel like speaking at church. Sometimes, when it is a beautiful day, I feel like I'd rather be bass fishing! Imagine all the problems I'd face if I went fishing when I didn't feel like preaching.

7. What do you think your life would be like if you lived every day based on your feelings?

_____

_____

_____

_____

Here's what I've learned about my own life. If I don't feel like forgiving, that's when I know I should probably forgive.

Galatians 5 talks about the fruit of the Spirit. One of the characteristics of the fruit talked about in Galatians 5 is self-control. Not emotions. Not feelings. Self-control. *[To learn more about the fruit of the spirit, check out the small group study "Juicy Fruit"]*

God equips us all with self-control, and we need to use it when it comes to doing the work of forgiveness. Read what God said about this part of forgiveness in Isaiah. Ⓨ-d

I, even I, am he who blots out your transgressions, for my own sake, and remembers your sins no more. Isaiah 43:25

This doesn't mean that God instantly forgets what we have done wrong. The miracle is that he *chooses* not to remember our sins.

The miracle about doing the work of forgiveness is not forgetting what someone has done to us; it's using God's grace and mercy to help us *choose* to forgive. Because when we remember it and choose to forgive, our memories can become memorials to the grace of God. We no longer look back at that situation and think, "I can't believe what they did to me!" Instead, we look back at the work of forgiveness and think, "I do believe what God did for me, and I choose to use that to forgive that person."

And the more we make those memorials, the sooner we won't think about the hurt or damage as much. That continues to free us up to be the kind of people that God desires. Ⓨ-**e**

DELIVER YOUR ENEMIES TO GOD

Finally, to unleash our unforgiveness, we need to deliver our enemies to God. We're to pray for our enemies. That is something that swims against the current of who we are. When I pray, here's how I would tend to pray. "God, show mercy to me, but deliver justice to them." That's what I want to say when I pray, but Jesus tells me to do something else.

> *But I tell you who hear me: Love your enemies, do good to those who hate you, bless those who curse you, pray for those who mistreat you. Luke 6:27-28*

When I love my enemies the way God asks, my entire perspective on the situation changes. I'm not excusing what they've done. I'm not acting like it didn't happen. But I am praying for them. I'm giving them to God. God is going to handle the situation inn his own way. And he is a much better judge than I'll ever be. When we give that situation to him, we no longer have to worry about it. It's a huge step of faith, but as you pray for your enemies great things will begin to happen.

8. Describe a time you took a relational issue in your own hands and it ended badly.

_____

_____

_____

_____

9. Describe a time you prayed for your enemies and God did something great.

_____

_____

_____

_____

When you put these four dimensions into action in your life, it will unleash you from your unforgiveness. You will let God turn you loose from those people sitting on your bench of unforgiveness. And you will experience a weight being lifted off you because you will no longer have to drag that bench full of people everywhere you go.

WRAP IT UP

This study has been an opportunity for God to do some powerful things in your life. I know God has opened your eyes and given you new insights into this powerful topic. And as you apply these biblical principles to your own life, God will continue to help you with any issue of unforgiveness.

10. During this study, what God-given principles of forgiveness have impacted you the most?

_____

_____

_____

_____

As we conclude this study, I have just one more question. Are you leashed up to unforgiveness? If so, ask God to unleash you. He wants to give you freedom because that freedom will allow you to walk in the fourth dimension of God's forgiveness—the supernatural dimension.

Prayer Requests:

_____

_____

_____

_____

_____

_____

_____

Notes:

_____

_____

_____

_____

_____

_____

_____

_____

_____

_____

_____

STEP IT UP

Take a step further over the next few days and spend some time reflecting on the following devotional thoughts that reinforce the previous session. Use these as reminders to take what you've learned and apply it to your everyday life.

DAY 1

John 20:19-23

If you have been trying the forgiveness thing for the past few weeks, you have probably discovered it is not easy. Remember that Satan will exploit any bitterness in your heart. He will not make it easy for you to do the work of forgiveness. Satan knows the unbelievable freedom that comes from unleashing unforgiveness and he is willing to fight to keep you from it.

When you are following God, it should not surprise you when you experience an obstacle. When you run into an obstacle making it more difficult to forgive, do not change paths. An obstacle is usually a sign that you are headed in the right direction. It could be a sign that Satan does not want you to continue with God's plan.

Following God requires commitment. When you run into obstacles on your path to forgiveness, do not try to find another path. Do not try to go around the obstacle. Conquer obstacles through the strength and power of God. Remember that Jesus gave the disciples the Holy Spirit before he gave them the task of forgiveness. If you try to forgive on your own strength you will not make it. Instead, ask for the help of the Holy Spirit.

Ask God to give you his strength to unleash unforgiveness in your life. If you have been trying to do this work on your own strength, commit this process to God and trust him to help you through it.

Notes:

_____

_____

_____

_____

_____

_____

_____

_____

_____

Prayer Requests:

_____

_____

_____

_____

_____

_____

_____

_____

_____

_____

_____

DAY 2

Luke 6:27-36

You have probably heard stories in the news about someone who has extended forgiveness to the man or woman who committed a terrible crime against them. You might even remember a serial killer receiving forgiveness from a family member of one of the victims. There are many stories like these, and each one is a beautiful picture of God's love.

These stories are beautiful because they are unique. As the verses you read today point out, we should not get credit for offering love and kindness to those who already love us. God says that beautiful love comes when we offer love to our enemies. Offering mercy to your enemies is rare and it's beautiful. God has been offering forgiveness to his enemies since the beginning of time. Anyone who has sinned has rebelled against God, chooses to be his enemy. But we have all been part of his beautiful forgiveness. Because of that, we can offer that same beautiful act to others.

Who opposes you? Ask God to show you how you could offer forgiveness to them.

Notes:

_____

_____

_____

_____

_____

_____

_____

_____

Prayer Requests:

_____

_____

_____

_____

_____

_____

_____

_____

_____

_____

_____

DAY 3

Luke 15:11-20

The son became tired of his father's house. He felt ready to set out on his own and experience life on his own terms. He broke his father's heart by asking for his inheritance up front, then leaving for a foreign country. While separated from his family, the son lived a selfish, foolish life and squandered all he had. The father worried about the fate of his son, hoping for the opportunity to see him again.

After living beyond his means, the son hit rock bottom. In desperation, he went back to his father to beg for a job so he could eat again. He didn't come back with the expectation of rejoining the family, but asked to be a servant so he could afford to live.

The father was put in a horrible position. Not only did he lose his son, but also he lost a significant portion of his estate. The son's decision took a huge toll on the father's emotional health. The father was left to feel the devastation of his son's decision. With all this hurt, the father was entitled to anger. The father was entitled to payback. The father was entitled to revenge for what his son had put him through.

Then, in the distance, the father saw the source of the anger, the one who caused so much hurt in his life. Sheepishly, the son was returning. A million thoughts must have gone through the father's mind in that moment. The hurt, the anger, the relief... all the feelings must have been fresh from the sight of his son. In that moment, the father left his entitlement, he left his dignity, and he left those who had been faithful to him. He ran to his unfaithful son.

He ran to embrace the object of his hurt. He ran to kiss the cause of his anger. He ran to forgive. This is what God did for us. We are the unfaithful child. If God did everything to forgive us, why can't we do that for others?

Notes:

_____

_____

_____

_____

_____

_____

_____

_____

Prayer Requests:

_____

_____

_____

_____

_____

_____

_____

_____

_____

_____

_____

DAY 4

Romans 12:18

This is a loaded verse. It leaves us with a great responsibility as well as great freedom. The responsibility is to live at peace with everyone. It is your responsibility. You are to take the initiative of peace whenever possible. You should be the one to suffer if it will lead to peace. You should be the one to sacrifice in the name of peace. That means accepting moments of humiliation, aggravation and insubordination. This is not an easy responsibility. God knew it would not be easy, but a reward he offers is freedom.

If you have done everything within your power to bring peace, you are free. You are free from the response of those who do not accept your offer of peace. You are free from the repercussions of those who choose to not follow God's plan. You are free to let it go.

God knew peace would not be an option that everyone would choose. He does not expect you to make other people choose peace. What he expects is for you to do everything within your power to make your relationships right. When you have done that, you are free. You do not have to carry it with you any longer. You do not have to drag the decisions of others with you. You are free to embrace the blessing for your obedience.

Have you done everything within your power for peace? If so, let it go.

FORGIVENESS 4-D FORGIVENESS

Notes:

_____

_____

_____

_____

_____

_____

_____

_____

Prayer Requests:

_____

_____

_____

_____

_____

_____

_____

_____

_____

_____

DAY 5

Isaiah 43:25

Most people struggle to balance their checkbooks. It is a burden to write down every expenditure and deposit. It is time consuming to check the bank statement every month and reconcile. It is not easy, so it is commonly avoided. Balancing checkbooks might not be common, but there is another registry we have an easy time balancing.

Everyone has a mental registry of offenses. We readily record every time someone offends us and remember the assigned hurt for every offense. We work the offenses in our mind and know just how much it will take to balance the forgiveness books. We know just what the other person owes us if they want to reconcile.

God wants us to put away our mental registry of offenses and follow his example. God was willing to "remember your sins no more." None of us have been offended as much as God. If he could do it, there is hope for every one of us. We do not have to seek justice for ourselves. We can let them go and trust God to take care of them. We can trust him.

Are you keeping mental records of the offenses others commit against you?

Whose offenses do you need to "remember no more?"

Notes:

_____

_____

_____

_____

_____

_____

_____

_____

Prayer Requests:

_____

_____

_____

_____

_____

_____

_____

_____

_____

_____

_____

COLLATERAL DAMAGE

LEADER'S NOTES

1. What is the most outrageous event you have witnessed?

-a

Have each student write their name on a sheet of paper. Then, below their name have them try to write their name with the opposite hand. Compare the two writings and discuss how unnatural it was to write with the opposite hand. There was a time when writing with either hand was unnatural for you, but through practice it became something you were able to do. Forgiveness will not be natural at first. But, if you will make a commitment to forgiving, you can begin to overcome the obstacle of it being unnatural.

2. Why do you think it is so unnatural to forgive someone who has hurt you?

The desire for revenge is something everyone experiences. It is stronger in some than others, but there is a breaking point that would make even the meekest of individuals want revenge. When someone hurts us, we want them to suffer at least as much as we have suffered. But, when we forgive we are taking the chance that the person who hurt us will not have to suffer. That goes against our desire for revenge.

Also, we all have a self-centered nature. This nature prompts us to look out for ourselves above all others. Combining that with the messages in society that "you will feel better if you get even" and "forgiveness is something you do only for the other person" makes forgiveness unnatural.

3. Without being specific, why are these people on your bench?

Tip: As your group is sharing, make sure to guard the identity of the people on the bench. Remember there are two sides to every story. You do not want to drag someone into the conversation without giving them the opportunity to share their side of the story.

As people are sharing, try to notice any common themes in their answers. It could be there are several key issues of unforgiveness in your group that will need to be addressed as the study goes on. By noticing these issues now, it can help you tailor your illustrations and the creative ideas for the needs of your group.

Ⓨ-b

Tip: Bring a video game controller to further emphasize this point. It is as if you give someone else the controls when you do not forgive them. For example, if you have an argument with someone at your lunch table then quit sitting at your lunch table because of that argument, you have just given that person your controller. Because of that unforgiveness you are being controlled by someone else.

What are other examples of how we can let others control us if we hold on to unforgiveness?

4. **Imagine you found out someone in your life had spread lies about you. If they came to you and asked for forgiveness, what would you do?**

   Tip: Some people in your group might feel uncomfortable sharing what they would really do in this situation. They may feel like they need to say the "church" answer since the entire study is on handling these type situations in a biblical way. Encourage everyone to be honest with the emotions they would feel in this situation. Let them know it is normal to be angry or hurt. It is even okay to express that anger and hurt as long as it does not compromise a biblical principle.

5. **What if that same that same person kept spreading lies about you? How many times do you think you could offer that person forgiveness?**

   Tip: Even the most kind and forgiving person has a breaking point. As people give their answers, ask them why? Why would they keep on forgiving that person so many times? Or, why would they not offer any more forgiveness. Some people in your group might feel they have been burned by offering forgiveness in the past so they are not willing to forgive now. Others might realize their continual need for forgiveness so they might be more willing to offer forgiveness. You could learn a lot about the condition of unforgiveness in your group from these answers.

6. **How do you think you would feel if you were late on your mortgage payments and your mortgage company called you up to say, "Don't worry about it. We'll take care of the rest you owe"?**

   Tip: After they have shared, ask your group for real life examples of this type of gift. It might not be as significant as having a mortgage paid, but the goal is examples of unwarranted kindness. Let your group share how this real life unwarranted kindness impacted them.

Ⓨ-C

Imagine you had been in a class where you were late turning in a lot of your assignments and made bad grades on the rest. You knew if you did not get an "A" on the final you were going to fail the class and have to repeat it in summer school. A couple days before the final, your teacher asked you to stay after class. You were expecting to get a speech about "trying harder" and "taking responsibility" but it did not go as you expected. Your teacher told you that based on your work you deserved an "F" but there was help for you. Your teacher then handed you a copy of your upcoming final with all the answers and told you to study it and help the rest of your class. How would that make you feel?

If that scenario happened to someone else, what would you think if they did not share the answers to the test?

If someone was given such a generous gift, you would expect them to share that generosity with others. It would seem ridiculous for that person to be selfish after they had received such generosity. That type of selfishness is a picture of how many treat God. They accept his generous forgiveness then refuse to share it with others.

7. Why do you think we so easily ignore how much we have been forgiven when it is our turn to offer forgiveness?

One problem is that we have a way of ignoring our own faults while being aware of the faults of others. An insulting word said by us might be seen as the result of a bad day while if that same insult was said to us it would be a horrible offense.

Also, there are times we do not think about our offenses against God in the same light as offenses against others. Since we do not have the tangible presence of God with us, it is easier to make light of those offenses. We are taught that everyone sins so this can lessen our sensitivity to sin. The result is we can ignore how many times we are forgiven by God.

8. When you think about how God has forgiven you, how does it make you feel about the unforgiveness you are leashed to?

Tip: The forgiveness of God can be hard to grasp so try the following visual. Think about the millions of dollars the wealthy king from Jesus' parable forgave. Try to imagine who large all that money piled up would be. Then, have them imagine the size of the few dollars the wicked servant would not forgive. Picture the two piles of money side by side. It seems ridiculous to hold on to something so small when you think about the amount that has been forgiven.

9. **How have you seen someone stay leashed to unforgiveness because of a self-deception barrier?**

   It is easy to stay leashed to unforgiveness. There are so many reasons that seem reasonable when we are in the heat of the conflict. Sometimes, the best thing we can do is to step back and try to look at our reason for staying leashed to unforgiveness from an outside perspective. This can be done by getting the advice of a trusted friend or a counselor. By taking on this perspective we can break the barrier of self-deception.

   Ⓨ-d

   What are excuses you have made for not forgiving others or asking for forgiveness?

   Ⓨ-e

   Have you ever noticed how revenge can get out of control quickly? For example, think about toilet paper or shoe polish wars. It starts out wrapping someone's house with about 12 rolls. The retaliation is getting wrapped with 50 rolls. The payback for that is getting rolled with 100 rolls, plus staking it down with plastic forks in the front yard. It does not take much to get out of control. Or, a car gets a few words shoe polished on the windows. The retaliation is windows getting completely covered in shoe polish. That escalates to shoe polish, cellophane wrap around the entire body so the doors will not open and the car on blocks. When you get into the revenge game, it will always end badly.

10. **What could you do to help you trust God and give him control of the person who wronged you?**

    Think about God's track record of faithfulness in the past. Consider the other "unnatural" things he has asked you to do that have proved good decisions. Then, be honest with God about your struggles of giving him control. Your honesty can free you up for God to overcome your fear. In your honest prayer, start praying for the person who wronged you. Do not just pray, "God, pay them back." Ask God to guide you as you pray so you can pray for their needs and other things that are going on in their lives.

    Ⓨ-f

    Think about prank shows like Punk'd. The funniest shows are when the people getting pranked will not let it go. We laugh at how foolish they look when they fight back and get angry causing more problems. They pout, cuss, fight and take it all personally. When they find out it was just a prank, they realize the ridiculousness of their actions. All of this could have been avoided if they had just let it go. Forgiveness can be one of the greatest tools for protecting your self-image. Learn to let it go before you see your actions for what they are and feel ridiculous.

FORGIVENESS COLLATERAL DAMAGE

ⓨ-g

Have you had knots in your stomach? Your pulse is racing, your breath is a little short, your mind is producing scenarios and responses at a lightning quick pace. Then there are those knots in your stomach, the twisting and turning as you get ready to face that person. Describe the way it feels to you when you have to do the forgiveness work.

Forgiveness is not easy. Most of us have a difficult time with it, but that does not excuse us from doing the forgiveness work God has called us to do.

CREATIVE NOTES

ICEBREAKERS

Name Game

Have each member write their name with their non-dominant hand. Compare the awkward signatures and find out how it felt to write with their non-dominant hand.

BRIDGE – Unleashing unforgiveness can be as unnatural as writing with your non-dominant hand. But, if we will commit to forgive, by God's strength we can accomplish the unnatural.

Stinky Question

What are some smells that gross you out? What is the worst thing you have found when you cleaned out your refrigerator?

BRIDGE – There are certain smells that can repulse others. Stored up unforgiveness can have the same effect in our lives.

Great Rivalries

What are great examples of rivalries throughout history? For example: Hatfield's and McCoy's, Yankees and Red Sox, celebrity feuds, etc.

BRIDGE – Some of the greatest rivalries in history started over insignificant matters. If the issues had been dealt with quickly, there is a chance they would have never reached rivalry status.

HANDS-ON ACTIVITIES

Writing Race

Pass out blank paper to members of the group then race to see who can write "I forgive you" seventy-seven times the fastest.

BRIDGE – Forgiveness should be a race. We should try to forgive as fast as we can, trying to cross the forgiveness finish line before bitterness and resentment can catch us (You could also use the completed papers as a visual reinforcement for forgiving 77 times).

Sweet Revenge

Break into several groups. Give all the groups a scenario where they were wronged then let them write out revenge plans making them as elaborate as wanted. Share the plans to see who had the best revenge plan. Then, discuss if those revenge plans would truly help deal with that wrong in the long run.

BRIDGE – Revenge can seem sweet at the time, but it is not a long term solution for the hurt and pain caused by others.

Extra Baggage

Load a piece of luggage until it is heavy. Pass the piece of luggage around and ask each member to pick it up and feel how heavy it is. As each person is feeling the weight of the luggage, discuss what life would be like if they had to carry that luggage every where they went.

BRIDGE – Unforgiveness weighs us down. God desires to lighten our load by teaching us to forgive.

VISUAL REINFORCEMENTS

Vinegar or Honey?

Set out a container of vinegar and a container of honey. Compare the tastes of the two items.

BRIDGE – Unforgiveness can be bitter like vinegar. God desires us to experience the sweet taste of forgiveness.

FORGIVENESS

Leash and collar

Place a dog leash and collar out so that everyone in the group can see it.
BRIDGE – We must be careful or we can get leashed to unforgiveness.

MEDIA REINFORCEMENTS

"Between You and Me" by DC Talk

This song shows the struggle of a person wrestling with their need for forgiveness.

"The Heart of the Matter" by Don Henley

An ex-boyfriend or ex-girlfriend deals with the reality that their "ex" is moving on. In trying to deal with the hurt, they find out the only way they can survive is to forgive. Forgiveness is the heart of the matter.

TAKE HOME OBJECT (Reminders of the lesson)

Leash

Pass out leashes with Matthew 18:21-22 written on them.

Chinese Finger Trap

Give Chinese finger traps from a party store as an illustration of how unforgiveness is a trap. We have the ability to get out of the trap if we will choose to let go.

OTHER

Can't Let Go

What is the longest you have held a grudge? How did that grudge start and why did you wait so long to let it go? What would it take now to let it go? What would it have taken when it first happened to let it go?

FORGIVE FOR GOOD

LEADER'S NOTES

1. How have you experienced freedom from unleashing your unforgiveness?

Freedom can come from not having unforgiveness consume your thoughts. There is the release of the emotional burden when you admit you were wrong. Sometimes, unleashing your unforgiveness can allow you to move on to new relationships or opportunities that felt blocked by unforgiveness.

Ⓨ-a

Have everyone stand in a circle facing each other. Everyone must reach across the circle and grab the hand of someone across from them until all hands are being held. Then, without letting go of any hand, try to get untangled.

Unforgiveness has a way of keeping us tangled up. When we trust God's plan we can be set free to live the life God designed for us.

Ⓨ-b

There are few things that go over and over in your mind like one of "those" songs. You know what songs are being talked about. They generally have simple lyrics, a catchy tune and lots of repetition. It may start out with you choosing to hum a little of the song. Before long you are singing the lyrics and enjoying the song. But then, things take a horrible turn. You begin to hear the song in your mind over and over again. Out of nowhere, you catch yourself humming or singing the song. By this point, the song has invaded you and there is no telling when it will come out again.

What are songs notorious for getting stuck in your mind?

Unforgiveness can become like a song stuck in your head. When you least expect it, you begin to sing that same resentful tune. It can pop up in all sorts of relationships. Before you know it, your resentment is poisoning other relationships for no reason. If you do not unleash your unforgiveness, the resentment can ruin other relationships.

2. How has a damaged relationship wreaked havoc on your emotions?

Damaged relationships can either create higher sensitivity or numbness. The heightened sensitivity creates hurt in abnormal responses to normal situations. For example, songs, places or people that remind you of the relationship could set off a volcano of hurt emotions just because of the heightened sensitivity.

On the other hand, some people let their emotions go numb after a damaged relationship. This is done to protect, but it actually decays. If you try to numb yourself against hurt, you will also numb yourself against hope. The result is like looking at paintings by Vincent van Gogh in black and white instead of the stunning colors of his original design.

3. How have you seen someone's hurt from one relationship damage other relationships?

The hurt from a previous relationship is still sensitive so normal conflicts in a new relationship irritate the old hurt. The result is the hurt will eventually be unleashed into the new relationship. The hurt is not just from the new conflict. The hurt is a combination of the new conflict and issues from the past. Also, the other person in the relationship can get hit with your hurt and have no ability to help because the hurt is from previous relationships. Your partner can have a sense of helplessness since they are trying to help you deal with hurt they had nothing to do with.

Ⓨ-c

Have you heard someone described as "damaged goods?" Maybe you heard someone described as "having issues" or "having a lot of baggage." These terms can come from not being able to let go. Maybe they were cheated on in one relationship so they bring trust issues to the next relationships. Maybe they were not treated well in one relationship so now they treat everyone else poorly. Those are examples of staying leashed to unforgiveness. If you stay leashed to unforgiveness you could end up as "damaged goods."

4. How do you think forgiving a person before they even ask for forgiveness could help mend that relationship quicker?

Mending a relationship after a conflict takes work. Being asked for forgiveness does not magically make all the issues disappear. There will still be work to be done even after someone asks for forgiveness. The work will either be done before or after the apology. If the work is done before, the relationship will obviously heal quicker.

5. How could practicing preemptive forgiveness be healthier for you than waiting for the person to ask for forgiveness?

The bottom line is the person may never ask for forgiveness. If you wait to be asked for forgiveness to start forgiving, you might never get to forgive. In that case, you will stay leashed to that unforgiveness forever. If you are waiting for the apology you are leaving a wound exposed. That wound will become infected by the experiences of life causing emotional, physical, relational and spiritual sickness.

6. In general, asking for forgiveness is never as bad as we imagine it will be. Why do you think we fear a strong reaction when we ask for forgiveness?

It is human nature to assume the worst. If you heard there was evidence that a celebrity was caught in a scandal, you would not assume innocence. For some reason it is easier to fixate on the negative. So, when we imagine a scenario of asking for forgiveness, it is easy to get caught up in how bad it could be.

Ⓨ-d

When have you been the most afraid to ask for forgiveness or give someone forgiveness? Explain your answer and if you were able to do the forgiveness work explain what helped you.

7. Practice apologizing in advance. It's a good idea to work out your conversation ahead of time. Tell the group what you might say if you were apologizing for hurting someone and let the group give you feedback. Let them tell you what they liked and disliked about your apology.

Tip: You might present scenarios for the apology. For example: how would you apologize for missing an appointment with a client? How would you apologize for forgetting the special day of someone you care about? How would you apologize for saying something out of anger to a friend, a family member, a competitor, etc?

Ⓨ-e

Figuring out when to go back and ask for forgiveness is not always an easy answer. It takes talking to other Christians and sometimes even counselors to find the right answer. As a group, try to figure out some general guidelines for going back to ask for forgiveness. For example: Don't ask for forgiveness if....

8. Admit to any of the following that applies to you. Because of unforgiveness, have you ever:
- Lost sleep?
- Felt sick to your stomach?
- Worried to the point of a headache?
- Experienced anxiety about being around someone?

Ⓨ-f

Just saying the words does not always show you are truly sorry. The Old Testament is full of principles for restitution. There were specific actions that accompanied the words "I'm sorry" to make up for what was done. In the New Testament, Jesus talks about repentance. It is the idea of doing a 180 degree turn away from what you were doing and choosing something new. In both cases, doing the forgiveness work required more than just saying the words.

In what situations do you think it might be appropriate to do more than just say, "Will you forgive me?" What do you think you should do in those situations to show that you are truly sorry?

9. What could you do as a Zaccheus-like response to God's forgiveness?

The key term in the Bible for responding to God's forgiveness is "repent." The term means to turn 180 degrees. The idea is that when you accept God's forgiveness you repent; turning in the opposite direction of what offended God. You do not stand dangerously close to what got you in trouble in the first place. You move away from the temptation and opportunity.

10. How could you combat the strategies Satan tries uses to prevent you from offering and receiving the forgiveness of God?

Prayer might be the standard church answer for problems, but that does not mean it is ineffective. Talk to God about what is going on and ask for his strength. Get your friends involved. Let them help encourage you to move through your unforgiveness and help you along in the difficult times. Also, think about the forgiveness you have needed in the past. This can cause you to offer forgiveness more readily than before.

CREATIVE NOTES

ICEBREAKERS

Meaning of Freedom

Ask the question, "When have you experienced true freedom" (paying off a debt, living on your own, etc.)? Or ask, "What does the word freedom mean to you?"

BRIDGE – Freedom can be a great experience and one way we can experience true freedom is when we forgive others.

Famous Forgiveness

What are examples of celebrities who had public offenses such as drug scandals, immorality, etc? How did the celebrities handle their offenses (did they apologize to the public or deny it)? Which celebrities were accepted back the quickest?

BRIDGE – There are few things the public will not forgive if forgiveness is asked for.

HANDS-ON ACTIVITIES

One, Two, Tie Your Shoe

Take turns performing simple tasks (like tying your shoes) but you can only do what someone else tells you to do.

BRIDGE – Staying leashed to unforgiveness gives others control over you. This can make even the simplest tasks difficult.

Salty Drink

Make different drinks and add a noticeable ingredient like salt to show how some things can work their way through the entire drink and ruin the whole thing.

BRIDGE – Resentment is a strong ingredient that can work its way through all aspects of our life and ruin it.

Let It Go

Give members paper and have them write what unforgiveness they are holding on to. Then wad it up and throw it away. Or, if you can find a safe environment you could light the wadded up papers on fire.

BRIDGE – God does not want us to hold on to unforgiveness. We must find ways to let go of unforgiveness.

VISUAL REINFORCEMENTS

Forgiveness Gift

Place a large gift wrapped box with the top off in front of the group. Let each member write the name of someone they are struggling to forgive on a slip of paper. Then, place the names in the gift wrapped box and put the lid on the box.

BRIDGE – Forgiveness is a gift we give ourselves and the people we forgive.

Rotten Fruit

Display rotten fruit in a large bowl.

BRIDGE – Unforgiveness can rot us emotionally, relationally, physically and spiritually.

Hamster Wheel

Set out a hamster wheel in the middle of the group.

BRIDGE – Replaying an offense in our mind, over and over again, is like getting caught in a giant hamster wheel. It will only wear us out and get us nowhere.

Lost Control

Have a video game set up where you control the character on the screen. Move the character around, manipulating them however you want.

BRIDGE – As you move the character on the screen, talk about how forgiveness puts the controller of your life in the hands of others.

MEDIA REINFORCEMENTS

"Stuck in the Moment" by U2

We can get stuck in unforgiveness and feel like we can't get out.

TAKE HOME OBJECT (Reminders of the lesson)

Stuck in Unforgiveness

Print the word "unforgiveness" and attach it to a glue stick or glue bottle. The glue reminds us that unforgiveness can have a negative bond on our relationships with others.

Freedom

Pass out small American flags with Job 5:2 attached as a reminder of the freedom in forgiveness.

Gift of Forgiveness

Give each person a small gift wrapped box as a reminder that forgiveness is a gift we give ourselves.

FORGIVENESS

Journal

Pass out 3" x 5" spiral notebooks. Encourage members to write down what and who offended them on one of the sheets of paper shortly after it happens. Then, tear the page out and throw it away as a reminder to give forgiveness issues to God. Also, the empty pages can be a reminder to keep a clean record when it comes to forgiveness.

OTHER

Forgiveness Tree

Find a tree (or similar object) that you can place your hands on every day before you go in your home. This represents placing those forgiveness issues in the tree for God to take. This will help keep from releasing that hurt on other people. Then, as you walk by the tree in the morning, notice how God has taken away what you have given him.

Luke 6:27-36

Discuss this passage in Luke. Talk about the difficulties of forgiving those who have wronged you. Also, what are practical ways you could "turn the other cheek?"

Fonzie Forgiveness

In the 1970's sitcom "Happy Days," there was the ultra cool Fonzie. In one episode, he had to admit he was wrong and ask for forgiveness. As he tried to say the right words, he kept getting stuck and stuttering on the words as if he was physically unable to apologize. It can be hard to do the forgiveness work, but God can enable everyone.

Worst Apologies

What are some of the worst apologies you have heard? In your opinion, what made them so bad?

BUILD A BRIDGE AND GET OVER IT

LEADER'S NOTES

1. What are some funny or embarrassing things you've experienced?

Tip: To add to this question follow up with what was learned from funny or embarrassing moments. We can hurt ourselves with unforgiveness, but we can also learn from that hurt.

Ⓨ-a

Have you ever had a two faced friend? Maybe the term "friend" should not be included because anyone who is two faced is not a friend. One minute they are kind to you and acting as if they like you, the next minute they are saying things behind your back. It seems so despicable to live in that hypocrisy. It hurts to have someone treat you that way. How could someone embrace you one minute and stab you in the back the next?

Unfortunately, we can be two faced to God when we embrace his forgiveness then hold on to unforgiveness against someone else. That is two faced and hypocritical. It must hurt God to see someone who has embraced his gift of forgiveness not offer forgiveness to others.

2. Share an example of how your own anger and resentment towards another person hurt your relationship with God?

Disobedience puts a strain on our relationship with God. We cannot fake God out. If we are rebelling in the areas of anger and resentment, he knows. That disobedience affects our ability to listen to God because we have put our agenda ahead of his. Also, it affects our ability to communicate because we have to make the area of our life with unforgiveness off limits. This keeps us from freely communicating the way God desires.

3. How is holding a grudge or not asking for forgiveness a selfish act?

Think about the barriers of forgiveness discussed in the first week: self-deception, self-defense, self-image, and self-protection. In each of these excuses for not forgiving, the focus is on us. Forgiveness could be something the other person needs much more than we do, but that is not taken into consideration because the spotlight is on us.

Ⓨ-b

A grudge may feel good at first, but in the end it can hold you back and hurt you. Have everyone stretch their arms straight above their heads and hold it. At first it feels good to reach up and stretch. As the pose is held, ask the group questions about holding grudges reminding them to keep their arms stretched above their heads. What were some of your greatest grudges? What started the grudges? What happened to keep those grudges alive?

After a couple minutes of talking about grudges with your hands above your head, your arms should begin to get heavy. This will change from just feeling heavy to starting to hurt. After a while, what initially felt good becomes a painful burden. That is a grudge. It might feel good at first, but it will end up hurting.

4. How could love help you overcome your grudge and help you become compassionate, kind, humble, gentle, patient and forgiving?

Think about God's definition of love. God loved so he created a perfect garden and fellowship for mankind. God loved so he rescued his people from enemies. God loved so he gave his Son. For God, love is sacrificial. Because God loves, he acts for the good of those he loves. If we "put on love" as God loves we will move past our selfish desires and reflect the characteristics God desires for the good of others.

5. How has holding onto unforgiveness emotionally drained you?

The theater of the mind is a powerful stage. We can be emotionally impacted by events that take place only on the stage of our minds. Have you ever woken up with your heart pounding, feeling exhausted from a nightmare? The event was only in your mind yet it impacted you. By replaying the offense and our plan of revenge on the stage of our mind we can wear out emotionally as if the event had actually happened multiple times.

6. In the following ways, how could you respond in anger without sinning?

- *An organization takes advantage of helpless people.*
- *Your friend is injured by a negligent driver.*
- *A co-worker spreads lies about you at work.*

In each of these events, we do not need to let our anger lead to physically assaulting or saying obscene things to the guilty party. We can boldly confront them without compromising the character of Christ. In the event of the organization you could write letters or organize a petition to try to bring change. For the negligent driver, you may not focus your anger on that specific driver as much as putting it toward an organization that fights against similar offenses. Just because you are a Christ-follower does not mean you have to go quietly into the night with your anger.

-c

The following are some student options for this question:
- *A group of bullies is picking on a helpless kid.*
- *A friend is injured in a car wreck by someone doing something stupid while driving.*
- *A person in your class starts lies about you that spread throughout your school.*

7. How have you seen unresolved anger dragged from one relationship to the next?

If you have ever been in a relational conflict and asked the other person, "Where is this coming from?" you could be experiencing unresolved anger. It has a way of creating or intensifying conflict in areas where there should not be conflict.

8. How have you seen Satan take a small situation and wreak havoc on an entire life?

"Then, after desire has conceived, it gives birth to sin; and sin, when it is full-grown gives birth to death" James 1:15. Satan has a way of planting small seeds of temptation that grow into imposing forces of sin. For example, most sex offenders do not start with sexual assault. Many start with something as socially accepted as pornography. Few drug addicts start with a needle or pipe. Their temptation came from legal buzzes that eventually lost their enticement. So, giving Satan a foothold in any area can be dangerous because he will try to take other areas.

-d

Unforgiveness keeps people from discovering God's greatness can happen several ways. The first is that a person had a bad experience with the church or a difficult experience in life and they blame God. They get mad at him and stay leashed to unforgiveness with God sitting on their bench. They will not give God a chance to show his greatness because they hold on to resentment from how they perceive God wronged them.

The second is that someone in a relationship with God will not extend forgiveness to others. They keep that resentment and anger in their hearts and it makes them callous to God's activity. They know God, but they are letting the resentment keep them from experiencing the greatness of God.

Finally, those people who know God but are not extending forgiveness to others can be a blockade for others seeing God's greatness. God works through those in a relationship with him to show others his love, compassion and forgiveness. There are people who want to believe in God's forgiveness, but they need someone to show them that forgiveness and it is not happening because God's representatives are harboring hurt.

9. What are a few things that could remind you to consider the cross when you are dealing with unforgiveness?

Regularly remembering the cross before you run into issues of unforgiveness is a great way to make sure you do not forget all God has forgiven you. Surrounding yourself with a core group of Christian friends can encourage you to remember the work God has done. Letting God use you in the lives of those who are entering into a relationship with him is another way to help you remember what God has done for you in the area of forgiveness.

10. What has helped you deal with resentment in your own life?

Tip: Out of the general answers, try to pull out principles that are universal. For example, if someone talked about how a friend from church helped them through resentment you could relate that to how important Christian relationships can be in dealing with unforgiveness.

-e

In that second group of people to forgive are parents. That can be a difficult group to forgive. Everyone knows parents are not perfect, but for some reason when they do something wrong it can be hard to stomach. Why do you think it can be so difficult to forgive your parents when they are wrong? Is there anything that has helped you forgive your parents?

11. What are excuses you have made to try to get out of asking for forgiveness?

"They probably don't even know I did something wrong."
"It would hurt them for me to bring it back up."
"It will be too difficult to track them down."
"I'm fine without forgiving them."

12. In times of competition, what has helped you keep from losing your cool in the heat of the moment?

Competition can bring out the worst in people. There is something about competition that creates tunnel vision on the prize. Winning and losing is not everything, and if we can beat that into our brains before the competition, we can avoid many embarrassing mistakes. If we cannot grasp that concept, maybe we should take a break from recreational competition until we can compete with the right mindset.

CREATIVE NOTES

ICEBREAKERS

In The News

Record and play a clip from the nightly news highlighting a heinous crime (murder, rape, kidnapping, robbery). Ask the group if they could forgive if the crime had been committed against them or someone they love. Ask team members where they draw the line when it comes to forgiveness.

BRIDGE —It's easy to talk about forgiveness when we look at other people's lives. However, when we become introspective, forgiveness becomes a much more complex issue. God wants us to unleash unforgiveness because it will allow us to move past the hurts to the blessings he has in store for our lives.

Band Aids®

Ask team members what "band aids" they place on unforgiveness instead of actually forgiving (i.e., not talking about the issue instead of truly letting go of it, re-telling the story over and over again).

BRIDGE —Holding on to unforgiveness places the perpetrator of our pain in the driver's seat and gives them control of our emotional well-being. Unforgiveness separates us from God. Jesus' sacrifice is the perfect example of forgiveness; we are called to forgive others when they wrong us.

Friend or Stranger?

Ask team members if it is easier to forgive someone they know or a stranger. Why? Further the discussion by asking if it is easier to ask for forgiveness or to give forgiveness, especially when you're still hurt.

BRIDGE —In Ephesians we are told "Do not let the sun go down while you're still angry." God challenges us to unleash unforgiveness even when it's hard. Only then can we experience the freedom that he desires for our lives.

Battle Scars

Ask team members to point out specific scars (i.e., on the arm, face, etc.), explaining how they healed and what lessons they learned from those injuries.

BRIDGE —We have all been injured in one way or another. Sharing our physical scars, the healing process, and the lessons learned can be therapeutic. Just as there is a natural process that heals our physical scars, the decision to unleash unforgiveness heals our emotional scars.

HANDS-ON ACTIVITIES

The Great Cover-Up

Print out several sheets of paper with the word "forgive" in a large font on each sheet of paper. Divide into groups of three or four and ask each group to write on band aids the excuses we make to avoid forgiveness. Then, try to cover the word "forgive" on the sheet of paper with the excuses we make for not forgiving. Compare the excuses we make between groups.

BRIDGE – Sometimes we try to cover up problems instead of doing the real forgiveness work. God wants us to truly forgive and not just put band aids on our problems. Only then can we experience the freedom of God's perfect plan for our lives.

Left Behind

Gather several newspapers prior to your meeting and ask each person to take a sheet of newspaper and crumple it up. Then ask them to take another and crumple it up. Continue this pattern through several sheets of newsprint. When everyone is through, ask them to inspect their hands.

BRIDGE – The ink remaining on team member's hands represents how an unforgiving spirit continues to build hate, resentment and bitterness. It leaves its mark on everything we touch. The cleaning of your group's hands after this exercise symbolizes the cleansing spirit of forgiveness.

Trick Candles

Serve individual cupcakes to the team, each one with a trick candle in the middle. Light everyone's candle and ask them to think about a person they need to forgive. Ask them to blow out their candle.

BRIDGE – Ask team members if their forgiveness is like the candle – we blow it out but it keeps coming back. If so, we are not doing the work of real forgiveness. When we choose to not completely forgive, we are mocking God's plan of forgiveness and breaking our fellowship with God.

A Bad Taste

Give each person in your group a piece of sour candy like a Sour Patch Kid® or Sour

Skittles®. Ask them to taste the candy then describe how that sour taste is like letting unforgiveness linger.

BRIDGE – Unforgiveness can leave a sour taste in our lives. God desires to remove that sour taste and let us taste his goodness (Psalm 34:8).

VISUAL REINFORCEMENTS

Key to My Heart

Place a lock and key on the table or in a central location where everyone can see it. Pose the question, "What do these two things have in common with forgiveness?"

BRIDGE – How ridiculous would it be to walk into a jail cell and lock the door behind us? Harboring unforgiveness puts us in bondage. We have the key to freedom and yet we choose to remain in jail. How much time do we waste in our personal jail cells before we realize that we had the ability to choose freedom all along?

Target

Draw a target on a sheet of paper making enough copies for everyone in the group. Have each member put names or events they need to forgive with the most difficult ones being in the bull's eye and the easier issues on the outer rings.

BRIDGE – Some issues of forgiveness are more difficult than others. When we unleash God's power in our unforgiveness we are able to hit the bull's eye of offering or receiving forgiveness.

Different Leashes

Purchase or borrow three different types of leashes: a choke leash, a regular nylon leash and a retractable leash and display them in the middle of your group.

BRIDGE – These leashes show different types of unforgiveness. Sometimes, when we hold on to unforgiveness it chokes the life out of us. Other times, unforgiveness is like a regular leash in that it is a constant companion. Then, some unforgiveness is like a retractable leash because we move away from it at times, but we are still connected in the end.

Pity Party

Provide small party favors and discuss how selfish it is to hold onto unforgiveness. It is as if we throw our own private pity party.

BRIDGE – When we hold on to unforgiveness, we place ourselves in the center of a big pity party. We spend time thinking about our hurts, licking our wounds and building up resentment toward others for the wrongs they have committed against us. This drains us emotionally, keeping us tethered to unforgiveness. Jesus died on the cross to forgive our sins – how can we possibly justify pity parties after what he did for us?

POSSIBLE MEDIA REINFORCEMENTS

"It's My Party and I'll Cry if I Want To" by Leslie Gore

The lyrics describe how a girl is wronged and decides that she wants to cry about it.

Les Misérables – 6:53 – 9:53

A priest welcomes a man into his home, only to be robbed by the thief. The priest offers forgiveness to the thief.

"We Bury the Hatchet" by Garth Brooks

Lyrics: "We're always diggin' up things we should forget about. When it comes to forgettin' baby, there ain't no doubt. We bury the hatchet but leave the handle sticking out." Some people do not truly forgive because they keep bringing it back up.

The Count of Monte Cristo – Track 29 (beginning of track to movie credits)

At the end of the movie, the main character realizes his quest for revenge is futile.

The Incredibles – Track 24

Mr. Incredible admits his mistake but his wife won't accept it. His response is "you keep trying to pick a fight but I'm just happy you're alive." There are times we would rather fight than forgive, but that does not settle anything.

TAKE HOME OBJECT (Reminders of the lesson)

Keys

Unlocking unforgiveness is in your control. When you have the key, you can let yourself out of the jail cell of unforgiveness any time you want.

Sour Patch Kids®

These can be a reminder of how bitter unforgiveness is and the effect it has on our soul.

Baby Rattle

Hand out baby rattles to remind us to not be selfish babies about unforgiveness.

OTHER

The Importance of an Apology

For some reason, it is especially hard to forgive if the other person has not asked for forgiveness. What do you think it is about an apology that affects our forgiveness so much?

Reservoir or River?

When it comes to forgiveness are you a reservoir or a river? Do you let God's forgiveness flow to you without letting it flow through you? If you do, then you are reservoir. God desires us to be a river of forgiveness. He wants to let his forgiveness run to us then through us to others.

4-D FORGIVENESS

LEADER'S NOTES

1. **Tell some of your forgiveness stories. What were some of your most memorable times asking for forgiveness?**

2. **How many times a month should you either have to forgive someone or ask for forgiveness?**

   We can view forgiveness as something that is done only for large offenses, but it happens on a daily basis. If someone bumps in to you or steps on your foot, you make a choice to forgive. You make a choice to forgive the person who cuts you off in traffic. The loud or annoying talker in your office is someone you forgive.

   Forgiveness does not have to be a grand display. It can be as simple as choosing to let it go. Think about all the little times of forgiveness, how often do you think you do the forgiveness work?

   (Y)-a

   Forgiveness does not just have to be for major issues. You forgive people for bumping into you in the hallway. There is forgiveness for someone cutting in line. If someone accidentally bumps into your desk you must choose to forgive them. Can you imagine what life would be like if you did not forgive anything? Life would be miserable if you held on to resentment for every little offense. Forgiveness is an unending and necessary part of life.

   (Y)-b

   Who are the people that help you with difficult situations? There are generally one or two people you can go to for advice or just to listen to you when you are facing difficult situations. God wants to be that "go to" person when you

121

have a forgiveness issue. That does not mean you cannot go to other people as well. Many times God will use your Christian friends to guide you into his will. But, God wants to be your final answer.

Think about it this way. When you are facing a difficult situation, you want to be partnered with the person that can help you the most. That is why deferring to God is brilliant. Who could help you more than the all-knowing, all-powerful, ever-present God?

3. What have you done to turn to God for help when you were unleashing unforgiveness?

It can be easy to leave God out of the areas we get hurt. He wants to be a part of those areas. He wants us to talk with him about those areas and be honest about what is going on. He wants us to invite him to work on those areas in our lives so we can experience his power and change. God offers his principles and promises through the Bible to meditate on and learn so we can be unleashed.

4. How has God helped you with unforgiveness?

God can work through other individuals to help us overcome unforgiveness. He can give them the exact words we need to hear to set us free. He can show us principles in his Word that allow us to overcome the unforgiveness in our lives. He can overcome thoughts that we could not get rid of.

Ⓨ-c

Why do you think it is so hard to be the person who takes the first step in repairing a relationship?

Taking the initiative is not easy. When you take initiative, you take risks. You risk being embarrassed. You risk being rejected. You risk being seen as weak for giving in to a conflict. You risk a lot when you take initiative, but you also risk a lot by not taking initiative. You risk prolonging unnecessary conflict. You risk emotional, physical, relational and spiritual damage. You risk missing out on what God has designed for you. There are risks both ways.

Taking initiative is a part of life. Think what life would be like without initiative. Practically every major invention came from someone taking initiative. They saw a need and took the initiative to find a solution. Millionaires were made by taking initiative. Great pieces of art, famous moments in sports and many other lasting impressions on society occurred because of initiative takers. It takes risk, but you could be risking more by not taking initiative.

5. How can you take the initiative when someone has wronged you?

Taking the initiative does not mean we have to confront the person who hurt us. Sometimes, the best thing we can do is to start processing our feelings before we talk with the person who wronged us. We can start praying for God's perspective and we might find out that we were not completely innocent. Then, if it is a good opportunity to confront the person who wronged us we are ready to settle it and not just seek revenge.

6. How does preemptive forgiveness (both in the sense of forgiving others and asking for forgiveness) relate to the verse you just read?

God calls to do everything we can, regardless of what other people do. Our decision to forgive should not be based on the words of someone else. Our decision to forgive or ask for forgiveness should come from an understanding of God's desire and a trust in him. There may never be peace with some people, but that does not mean God will withhold peace in our lives if we will do all that depends on us.

7. What do you think your life would be like if you lived your life based on your feelings?

Tip: Ask for things they do on a daily basis that they do not feel like doing. Many of the things we do not want to do are some of the most important things we do. If we quit doing those things, we would suffer far more than the self-control it takes to do what God has called us to do.

ⓨ-d

Look at the following list of emotions and write down several different emotions on separate slips of paper: confusion, anger, surprise, happiness, pity, love, fear, hope, jealousy, grief, paranoia and rage. Fold the slips of paper and put them in something you can pass around and draw out of. Each person has to react to the following scenario with the emotion they draw.

Months ago, you and your best friend decided to work together to win tickets to your favorite band's concert. The deal was, whoever won the tickets would share with the other person. Your friend won the tickets so the two of you started making plans for the concert. On the day of the concert, your friend is late picking you up for the concert. You call but get no answer. You start to get nervous because the concert is about to start and you still have not heard from your friend. You finally get a phone call from your friend and you can hear loud music in the background. Your friend explains that they decided to take someone else to the concert and hopes you are not too upset.

ⓨ-e

What are some of the most impressive acts of forgiveness you know? What makes those acts so impressive in your opinion?

8. Describe a time you took a relational issue in your own hands and it ended badly.

Tip: As in other discussions of offenses, leave the names of the offenders out. Focus on the actions of the person answering. Try to pinpoint how closely the bad result is connected to the actions of the person answering the question.

9. Describe a time you prayed for your enemies and God did something great.

Greatness does not have to be that the other person changes. Sometimes the greatest thing God can do when we pray for our enemies, is to change us.

10. During this study, what God-given principles of forgiveness have impacted you the most?

Tip: Encourage your group to take time to look through their studies to notice the parts that impacted them the most. It could be a specific statement that changed their perspective and consequently their actions. Or, it could be applying the forgiveness principles and getting to be unleashed from certain people on the bench of unforgiveness.

To give your group a chance to think about their answers, come prepared to share what part of the study impacted you the most.

CREATIVE NOTES

ICEBREAKERS:

Skills

Name one skill you had to work at to acquire.

BRIDGE – We are willing to invest time and energy in areas we value. What about forgiveness? It's not natural to forgive; forgiveness is a skill that we must practice over and over again in order for it to become a constant in our lives. Are you willing to make the investment to grow in this area of your life?

Conviction

Ask team members to share a time when they were convicted to say "I'm sorry."

BRIDGE – Even when we don't feel like forgiving others, God has a plan to help us reach the goal of forgiveness. By choosing to enter the fourth dimension and follow God's plan of deferring to him, deciding to take the initiative, disengaging from our emotions and delivering our enemies to him, we are supernaturally energized to unleash unforgiveness in all areas of our life.

Draw the Line

Ask team members if in today's society there are any unforgivable sins.

BRIDGE – As Christians, we are called to forgive without limitation. God directs us to love our enemies and to pray for those who mistreat us. Only by living in the land of 4-D forgiveness can we overcome the resentment and bitterness associated with "unforgivable sins." Choosing to do it God's way opens the door for God to accomplish miraculous events in our life.

HANDS-ON ACTIVITIES

Emotional Craziness

Write emotions like "confusion, anger, surprise, happiness, pity, love, fear, hope, jealousy, grief, paranoia and rage" on separate slips of paper then fold them up and put them in a hat to be drawn. Explain a scenario where you have just found out your best friend has been lying about you and you confront your friend. Then, let people show how they would respond based on the emotion they drew out of the hat.

BRIDGE – God wants us to show self-control in our lives. If we are not careful, we will react with whatever emotion comes up that day and it may not be the appropriate emotion.

Right Tool for the Job

Try to do a simple task without the right tools. For example, remove a nail or a screw in a board with a pair of tweezers. Then, give the right tool for the job and discuss how much easier it was.

BRIDGE – Forgiveness is hard work! We can try as hard as we want, but we will not be able to accomplish unleashing unforgiveness on our own. Jesus sent us the Holy Spirit, a powerful tool in our lives, and we must rely on his presence and strength to accomplish the work of real forgiveness in our lives.

A Reminder to Forgive

Ask team members to write on a note card someone they would like to forgive and why they want to forgive them. Have them seal the card in a self-addressed envelope then mail them out the following week.

BRIDGE – Many times we experience the desire to forgive, but it is easy to let that desire pass without acting. God desires us to act when we feel prompted to forgive so we can be unleashed.

VISUAL REINFORCEMENT

Fruit of the Spirit

Put out a fruit display to remind us to try to keep the fruit of the Spirit in our lives.

Theme Night

Organize your team meeting so that you can have a theme night. Choose key reinforcements from the lesson (peace signs, lasagna, etc.) and have the meeting be a celebration of the fourth dimension.

BRIDGE – Experiencing the freedom and joy of unleashing unforgiveness could be as close as one decision away. The decision to follow God's plan of living in the fourth dimension is within our reach – we just need to choose to grasp it.

MEDIA REINFORCEMENT

"I Just Wanna Be Mad" by Terri Clark

Lyrics: "I'll never leave, I'll never stray. My love for you will never change, but I ain't ready to make up." We can be tempted to stay mad, but the longer we hold on the greater the chance we will stay permanently leashed to unforgiveness.

You've Got Mail – 1:39:10 – 1:41:19

In this conversation Tom Hanks says, "I put you out of business so you're entitled to hate me." Meg Ryan's response is "I don't hate you." and Tom's response to that is, "But you'll never forgive me – you're too proud."

"If I Know Me" by George Strait

Lyrics: "But if I know me, I'll turn this car around. I won't get halfway through town and I'll be sorry. I'll stop and call, and you'll say you're sorry too, and I'll come runnin' back to you, if I know me." We need to be the type of people who take the initiative to forgive.

TAKE HOME OBJECT

Peace

Purchase small peace tokens or charms and ask team members to carry them around with them as a reminder to constantly unleash unforgiveness and choose to live in peace.

Put a label on an Energizer battery or package of batteries that says: "Forgiveness: keep giving & giving & giving."

OTHER

Emotions of Forgiveness

Ask the group what are some emotions they feel when they ask for and receive forgiveness (i.e., relief, peace, release, unburdened). What emotions do they feel when they harbor unforgiveness (i.e., resentment, anger, bitterness, distracted, stress)?

Living in Peace

The Bible calls us to live in peace whenever it depends on us. What are examples of when living in peace has not depended on you? What did you do in that circumstance?

The Table

Casting The Vision For The Local Church

The foundational series for small groups by Ed Young uniquely relates different aspects of eating a special meal to our purpose as Christ followers. As we focus on serving others, it reminds us in a powerful way that there's always room at the table.

The Creative Marriage

The Art Of Keeping Your Love Alive

Disposable relationships and throw-away marriages permeate our culture. When the dream fades and the realities of life set in, many just throw in the towel. In this six-week study, Ed speaks openly and honestly about the hard work involved in a creative marriage and the lasting rewards of doing it God's way.

In The Zone

How To Live In The Sweet Spot Of Success

Do you want to live a life in marked contrast to those around you? In this study, Ed Young shares powerful biblical principles about what it means to live a life blessed by God—to live *in the zone*.

Snapshots of the Savior

Jesus—Up Close And Personal

So often when we think of Jesus' life, our photo album is limited and sketchy. In this powerful study of talks, Ed Young shares vivid images from the Bible to help provide a broader, panoramic view of Christ's mission and ministry.

Mission Possible

Everyday Leadership Principles For Everyday People

With an impossible mission before him, Nehemiah allowed God to develop him as a leader and to give him the skills and character necessary to carry out his mission successfully. This study uncovers the timeless leadership principles found in this Old Testament power struggle between conniving political leaders and a persevering construction mogul.

X-Trials – Takin' Life to the X-Treme

An Extreme Study In The Book Of James

In this book, *X-Trials*, Ed Young leads you through a verse-by-verse look at one of the most challenging and controversial books of the Bible, the book of James. Living life as a Christ-follower in today's world requires extreme faith!

Character Tour
A Biblical Tour Of Some Great Characters With Great Character

Certain character qualities stand out in notable characters throughout the Bible. In this creative series, Ed Young uses those great biblical role models to help us crack the character code and become people who live out godly character from the inside out.

Virtuous Reality
The Relationships Of David

People in your life can pull you up or drag you down. Join this journey into the life of David as we discover how this "man after God's own heart" lived out the daily reality of his relationships. By uncovering the good and bad in your relationships, Ed Young will help you discover how to honor God regardless of who crosses your path.

Ignite
Refining And Purifying Your Faith

Fire, it is a source of destruction and a source of life. It incinerates and destroys. But it also refines and purifies. In the Bible, God used fire and other trials to turn up the heat and reveal His power through the lives of people. Ed Young explores these trials from Scripture to help fan the flames of our own faith today.

Tri-GOD
Understanding The Trinity

Three in One, One in Three. The Trinity. God in three persons—Father, Son, and Holy Spirit—is one of the most misunderstood doctrines in the Christian church. Yet Ed Young teaches in this exciting new series that our awareness of God's triune nature is pivotal to growing with Him.

First and 10
The Whats, Whys And Hows Of The Ten Commandments

Where do we find our moral foundation in this game of life? In a world of ever-changing culture, circumstances, and philosophies it all goes back to the big ten. Ed Young will take you on a thought-provoking, soul-searching look at the Ten Commandments.

Wired for Worship
Make Worship A Part Of Your Every Day Life

There is great debate and misconception surrounding "worship." One thing holds true, as human beings we are wired for worship. Whether it is career and finances or relationships and family, we instinctively worship something. Join Ed Young as he dives in to discover what it means to truly worship God in your life.

Praying for Keeps
A Guide To Prayer

Imagine how awesome it would be to sit down and have a face-to-face conversation with God! In the small group study, you will learn how you can effectively and naturally communicate with God. Ed Young will walk you through the biblical principles that will guide you into a more intimate and rewarding life of prayer.

Fatal Distractions
Avoid The Downward Spiral Of Sin

In this in-depth study, Pastor Ed Young makes a frontal assault on the seven deadly sins that threaten to destroy our lives.

Marriage Unveiled
Components Of A Healthy, Vibrant Marriage

This dynamic study uncovers the essential elements that will keep you growing together for a lifetime. Through this straight-forward, no-holds-barred approach, you will experience help and hope for troubled marriages as well as a challenge to make great marriages greater.

RPMs - Recognizing Potential Mates
Supercharge Your Dating Life

Whether you're a single adult, a student, or a parent, this creatively driven study will provide foundational principles on how to date and select a mate God's way. We're going to cruise past the cultural myths and embark on a supercharged ride to the ultimate relational destination.